Where It All Went Wrong

Where It All Went Wrong

The Case Against John Howard

AMY REMEIKIS

SCRIBNER

First published in Australia in 2026 by Scribner,
an imprint of Simon & Schuster (Australia) Pty Limited
Level 4, 32 York St, Sydney NSW 2000

New York Amsterdam/Antwerp London Toronto Sydney/Melbourne New Delhi
Visit our website at www.simonandschuster.com.au

10 9 8 7 6 5 4

A catalogue record for this book is available from the National Library of Australia

9781761822117 (paperback)
9781761822131 (ebook)
9781761822124 (audiobook)

Cover design by Laura Thomas
Cover image: Dean Treml (Getty Images)
Typeset by Midland Typesetters, Australia
Printed and bound in Australia by Griffin Press

The paper this book is printed on is certified against the Forest Stewardship Council® Standards. Griffin Press holds chain of custody certification SCS-COC-001185. FSC® promotes environmentally responsible, socially beneficial and economically viable management of the world's forests.

To Phyllis from Brisbane who was right
and my Tete who was wrong.

And to Riddley, Hugo, Wolf and all the children –
may we fix *gestures to everything* for you.

Contents

Introduction

Lest the critics say there is not a positive word for John Winston Howard in this book, let's start with some.

Howard was perhaps Australia's most influential and effective politician, at least in modern political history. He is the Liberal Party's Whitlam, changing the country in ways we are still reckoning with.

Howard had the patience of Moses, the tenacity of Churchill and the cunning of Odysseus, all wrapped up in the most bland, benign and white package you could imagine. He understood one of the most important lessons in politics, and life – people believe the story you tell them.

The story Howard spun was so powerful he had people voting against their own interests for years – and thanking him for it.

And that's where the positive words end. Indeed, they're only positive if you feel that the gaining and retention of power are laudable irrespective of what you do with them. It's one of the many strange outcomes of the Howard Years (March 11, 1996 to December 3, 2007) that even his opponents over time have felt compelled to praise his political skills even as they decry the consequences, so that the greatest legacy of this 'conviction' politician has in fact been decisively to separate politics and conviction, means and ends. The purpose of this book is to bring the ends back into focus, because we're still living with the consequences of Howard's convictions.

Above all, John Howard was not afraid of using power and in fact wielded it to shape the nation to his desires. Howard stomped over decades of industrial action, social norms and progress, making Australia smaller, individualistic and in many senses crueller, without taking a backward step. He convinced a generation that they were entitled to be 'relaxed and comfortable': if you weren't relaxed and comfortable, well, that was probably your own fault and you just didn't deserve what John Howard could give you. Howard convinced a nation that thinking about politics was what was wrong with politics.

If that meant history had to be ignored and, in some cases, entirely re-written, to avoid uncomfortable truths, so be it. The future was to be ignored entirely. In pursuit of a complacent present, Howard changed how we think about each other, ourselves, the economy, what our country owes us, our history, the acceptable bounds of social discourse, multiculturalism, what and who matters, and what we are capable of as a nation. But not for the better.

You can trace almost every major societal issue Australia is facing today to Howard and his vision. He was either at the centre of it or laid the foundations for it. If you want to know the answer to who fucked millennials and gen Z, the answer is easy: Howard.

Howard persuaded Australia to see itself through the lens of his own arrested development. The Australia of his youth, led by the Liberal prime minister and founder of the modern Liberal Party, Robert Menzies, seemed to establish itself as a Pleasantville in Howard's mind, something to be recreated no matter the cost. As a result, Howard set about recasting something that only truly existed in the eyes of a middle class, methodist, white child in 1950s suburban Australia – which Howard translated into 'ordinary' Australia, for 'ordinary' Australians.

He convinced millions of people that his values were *their* values, and those shared values meant he understood them, and what he wanted was what they wanted. No matter what the policy, Howard tied it back to 'values', which by the year 2000 had been reduced to four pieces of jingoism: 'self-reliance, a fair go, pulling together, and having a go'.[1]

But Howard destroyed the 'fair go'. He made it harder to 'have a go' – ripping apart the social safety nets, privatising essential services and turning houses into a source of wealth, over and above the right to shelter. His version of self-reliance didn't apply to the nation itself, which he tied ever closer to the United States, proudly allowing a sovereign nation to become the 'deputy' of a declining world power. Pulling together meant ostracising those who did not agree with a conservative world view, marking them as 'elites' or 'un-Australian', helping to tend to the seeds of division that continue to flourish today.

'No one owns the national identity,' said Howard in 1995. He then spent the next twelve years setting the boundaries for what an acceptable national identity was. The year before he was elected, Howard accused the Keating government of being 'living proof of the Orwellian dictum that those who seek to control the future first try to control the past by distorting it for their own particular narrow purpose'.[2] If we are to apply the notion that every accusation is a confession, Howard outlined how he would govern as prime minister in that one single sentence. He rewrote our past to control the future and set about limiting who was worthy of cultural empathy.

And he won.

Successive Labor governments largely gave up trying to unpick what Howard put in motion and instead just folded in his visions into their own policy blueprints. And the Liberal Party is now reaching its inevitable, catastrophic conclusion to Howard's vision. Howard was the first elected Australian prime minister to describe himself as a conservative, and while much has been made of the 'broad church' he held together in the Liberal Party tent, it's clear to see how his influence set the party on its current course. Tony Abbott, Scott Morrison and Peter Dutton are all creations of Howard. Each more craven than the last, they collectively reduced the Liberal Party to a culture war smokescreen, standing for nothing beyond the current leader's predilections and the reverberations from increasingly rabid echo chambers. In fact, the only thing that may be worse off for Howard's stewardship than the nation itself is the Liberal Party he fought so hard to rule. Lazarus with his triple bypass may have risen, but nothing will save the Liberal Party.

Howard's attacks on 'elites', his elevation of 'special individuals, not special interests' for the country as a whole, his casual qualifier of 'deserving of help' when talking of the need to look after the less fortunate, his lionising of 'traditional' families, seem tame when viewed through today's tarnished and battered lens, but it started the shift from the collective to the individual in Australia, and in doing so made us all the more vulnerable to the divisive messages of today.

Howard was a conviction politician, which meant he never bent on the issues he cared about. He didn't care about every issue – and that's where he let the politics play out as it did, which is where some of the myth of his 'broad church' takes root – but if it was something he wanted done, he made it happen. No matter the cost. It's how he won a lot of what he wanted – the sale of Telstra, pushing through the GST. If something got in the way like a pesky election vow, then he would just invent something else like the concept of 'core and non-core promises' to get his way. Howard was driven by his own values and what he wanted to change he did, no matter how hard it may have been. And he truly didn't care about what he didn't care about. Some took this to mean he listened to his Cabinet, or his voters, and was willing to back down if persuaded otherwise. But that is a very surface-level take. Looking back on Howard's career it is clear that he was a master of playing politics, he knew how to keep his rivals busy fighting each other and never once bent on anything he truly wanted. But he was just so pleasant about it, bumbling around in tracksuits like an off-duty Mr Sheen, that it was easy to miss just how *good* he was at getting his own way. It kept him in power, unchallenged, for eleven years, but also meant he could railroad his way into changing the country to suit himself. And he did, unapologetically.

Howard narrowed the boundaries of what it was to be an Australian and often made our political debate more cruel. His government muffled critics, silenced scientists, scared the public service and punished dissenters. Today's far-right culture warriors have their 'war on woke'. For Howard, 'political correctness' was to blame for everything from multiculturalism to the bid to formally cut Australia's ties from the British Empire, to Indigenous self-determination, to a foreign policy orientating towards Asia rather than to America as he wished. Any progress Australia had made in addressing its racist and xenophobic history was pushed back decades by Howard, who made border policies one of the nation's most successful exports. He not only gave cover for a growing far-right wing, he helped it flourish. He sent us to war on a lie, for the benefit of another nation. He divided us into deserving and not-so-deserving. He's a big part of the reason everything, and I mean everything, is harder than it should be. Owning a home. Getting ahead. Finding acceptance for your identity. Aged care. Health care. Wages growth. Population growth. Foreign policy. Mapping out a future, both as individuals and a nation.

And he never truly went away.

Far from being 'Honest John' or even Beige John, Howard is, in short, where it all went wrong.

1
Culture Wars

> 'I think in public life you take a position and I think particularly of the positions I've taken in the time I've been prime minister. I have to live with the consequences of those both now and into the future. And if I ever develop reservations, well, I hope I would have the grace to keep them to myself . . . you take a position and you've got to live by that and be judged by that – and that's my position.'[1]
>
> John Howard, 2006

That was John Howard's response to a question from journalist David Speers in November 2006, as his first visit to Vietnam as prime minister was concluding. Speers, then with Sky News, now with the ABC, had wanted to know if Howard – who had spent most of the trip talking up Vietnamese–Australian relations without mentioning, you know, the war – thought Australia's involvement in the Vietnam war was a mistake.

Reading the transcript, you can sense Howard's mind turning. His answer reveals more than just how he felt about Australia's involvement in a war that, historically, has been viewed as a mistake. It also shows a prime minister unwilling to admit he is wrong – ever. If anything, he was trying to make a virtue out of denying he changed his mind, even if, indeed, he ever had.

Howard made up his mind *a lot* about the sort of Australia he wanted us all to live in – not just policies for prosperity, but the *kind* of place he thought the country ought to be. Even as we live with the increasingly dire consequences of that national vision, Howard has not taken a backward step, even deep into his retirement. And therefore neither have those who venerate his memory. To understand why so many conservatives in Australia are addicted to fighting culture wars, and how those wars have been weaponised as a divisive distraction tool, you need not look further than Howard.

'The times will suit me,' Howard told journalist Anne Summers in July 1986. Eventually he was right, but as Summers wrote in 2003, not because Australia suddenly became conservative, but because of the work Howard put in to shape the times.[2] He's been doing it ever since, either directly, through his interventions in friendly media, or by proxy, through his advice to protégés who have continued to wage the wars for him.

Having spent most of Australia's most socially progressive years, between the 1960s and 1980s, in the political wilderness, as soon as he was elected Prime Minister in March 1996, Howard set about cultivating an Australia that rejected the self-directed sovereignty path it had been set upon, in the three main areas of reconciliation with its Indigenous populations, unshackling itself from the British monarchy and turning towards Asia. (Probably not unexpected for someone who once named Bob Dylan and Joan Baez as his favourite vocalists, but notably not for the lyrics they were vocalising.)

Howard also saw no issue with this, telling Liz Jackson during the 1996 election campaign 'you shouldn't get so hung up, you shouldn't be so politically correct, that somebody that may not necessarily share the views of the vocalist, can't enjoy the music, that's very narrow-minded. That's the sort of thing that you'd expect from the politically correct brigade.'[3]

So it is not surprising that someone who liked a protest song purely for the guitar strumming and sweet voices would seek to derail Australia becoming a republic as one of his first goals. Tradition obviously isn't 'politically correct'. To make that happen, Howard began attacking socially progressive policies and made sure to centre his version of the past as much as possible. He also successfully carried out a personally favoured political move of his – divide and conquer – which the republican supporters not only fell for but allowed to dictate most of their campaigns.

Indigenous self-determination was sacrificed to make that happen.

Still, in 1996, after decades of inching towards it, Australia was on the path of formal national reconciliation, with the 1991 passage of the *Council for Aboriginal Reconciliation Act 1991*. The vision was for a 'united Australia which respects this land of ours; values the Aboriginal and Torres Strait Islander heritage; and provides justice and equity for all'.

The following year in 1992, the High Court handed down its Mabo decision, which overturned the legal fiction of *terra nullius* and recognised native title, and Paul Keating delivered his Redfern speech, admitting 'it was we who did the dispossessing. We took the traditional lands and smashed the traditional way of life. We brought the diseases. The alcohol. We committed the murders. We took the children from their mothers.'[4]

Australia was on the path to a national apology, or at least more broadly, a recognition of the original sin of settlement, of which an apology would be an important part.

But that did not fit into Howard's view of Australia's past, or where he wanted to take the country. Keating's proclamation of 'we', as in settler Australians, became 'them' and 'us' under Howard; them being those who agreed with Keating's views of reconciliation and blame acceptance and 'us' being anyone who felt it was all a bit too much.

Howard's views were clear in the election campaign. In an interview with the ABC's Liz Jackson, he described himself as 'direct', 'unpretentious' and 'pretty dogged' and able to have a laugh at himself. Asked to describe himself in three words, he responded 'an average Australian bloke. I can't think of a nobler description of anybody than to be called an average Australian bloke.'[5]

But when it came to values, and how he wanted to shape the nation, Howard didn't budge.

In that same interview, when asked to give his vision for the year 2000, Howard told *Four Corners*: 'By the year 2000 I would like to see an Australian nation that feels comfortable and relaxed about three things. I would like to see them comfortable and relaxed about their history. I would like to see them comfortable and relaxed about the present and I would also like to see them comfortable and relaxed about the future.'

The average Australian bloke ought – *deserved* – to be comfortable and relaxed. He went on: 'You can't possibly hope to feel excited about something unless you feel comfortable and familiar with it.' (A remarkably revealing definition of excitement.) 'If you really want to drive Australians away from interest in something, you disturb their sense of comfort about it, and you succeed in driving them away from it.' (So Australians are quite naturally by definition uninterested in anything uncomfortable.)

'It is very important we don't, as a nation, spend our lives apologising for the past.'

And so, he never did. Howard had constructed an Australian identity impregnable to all but the most tectonic change. One for which a new or even tweaked idea was, in fact, un-Australian.

In 1997, he revisited his vision of relaxed and comfortable in more detail:

> No society which has a proper understanding of its history or its present or an apprehension and belief about its future can deny certain blemishes and great historical wrongs and Australia, of course, is no exception. But I used that phrase because of a deeply held belief I have about Australian nationalism and Australian patriotism and that is that we should not find ourselves engaged in a frantic and constant search for a new or a different identity. We should not allow ourselves to lapse into a perceptional seminar about our identity. There is a very identifiable Australian character and Australian identity. It's very different from what it was forty or fifty years ago although there are some common threads that bind the Australian identity of today with the Australian identity of fifty years ago.
>
> When we examine our national identity we should always remember that the symbols that we hold very dear as Australians and the beliefs that we have about

> what it is to be an Australian are not things that can ever be imposed from above by political leaders of any persuasion. They are not things that can be generated by self-appointed, cultural elites who seek to tell us what our identity ought to be. Rather they are feelings and attitudes that grow out of the spirit of the people.[6]

Here we have the essence of Howard, raising several issues we'll return to in due course. The two that concern us here are first, the idea that leadership is impossible – 'Australians' know what they believe and only need a government that stops anyone telling them different. And second, that identity is not 'perceptional' – it somehow exists, independent of what we think it is, or is not. And what is it? Howard believed Australians emerged from 'great traumatic events' such as Gallipoli and 'those other things that through long usage and custom and a feeling that suits the temperament of the Australian people we have come to love and to hold dear'. Whatever *they* are. But the point was, the past is the past, and the only things we need to hold on to are the things that made us feel good about being Australian.

It was a massive departure from Keating's rousing call for accountability. Howard didn't think his Australia needed to be accountable for anything. Especially its past.

Besides Gallipoli, the other specific thing Australians axiomatically 'love and hold dear' was cricket. Howard dedicated much of his first Australia Day speech as prime minister to cricket legend Don Bradman, framing January 26 to once again be about the Australians he wanted celebrated.

Cricket, especially Test cricket, and especially Bradman's cricket, became of utmost importance to Australia's identity under Howard. Which from the view of 2026 seems strange as cricket lovers fight to maintain Test cricket relevancy in a Big Bash/IPL world. But it goes to show just how much of a chokehold Howard had over the culture. His heroes became the nation's heroes, even if you had to dig into the history books to find them.

What's the one thing all those heroes had in common, you ask? They were 'us' – the Australians Howard wanted us all to emulate. And if you weren't us, then you were 'them'. And on the culture war battlefield, being one of 'them' was among the worst things you could be labelled.

All of that was evident from the beginning. As the newly elected prime minister, Howard went on the ABC's *7.30 Program* and held up a map of Australia with 78 per cent of it shaded brown, claiming that the recent Wik High Court decision, which established native title rights, gave Indigenous Australians 'veto' power over most of Australia (to be discussed further in Chapter 4). It wasn't true then, or now, or even meaningful (because what on earth could a 'veto' power even mean?) but it immediately started the damaging myth that Indigenous Australians could 'come and take your house'.

Howard then opened the 1997 Australian Reconciliation Convention – an event that was years in the making, organised by the Council for Aboriginal Reconciliation (now Reconciliation Australia) and designed to establish and discuss Indigenous issues and a way towards reconciliation as a nation – by dismissing the dispossession of land and the murder of their people as insignificant. Why? Because most Australians didn't want to believe it. Howard stated:

> In facing the realities of the past, [. . .] we must not join those who would portray Australia's history since 1788 as little more than a disgraceful record of imperialism [. . .] such an approach will be repudiated by the overwhelming majority of Australians who are proud of what this country has achieved although inevitably acknowledging the blemishes in its past history.[7]

The delegates rightly turned their backs on him. Howard didn't take offence – to him, this was proof the 'politically correct' elites needed to be put back in their place through the 'common sense' of ordinary Australians. He did it over and over and over again.

With Pauline Hanson, then a recently dis-endorsed Liberal candidate, dropped for racist comments against

Indigenous people, whipping up the right flank and calling it 'free speech', which Howard benefited from – a clean hands approach to stirring discontent – Howard doubled down on what became the 'history wars', adopting the phrase the 'black armband' view of history, which historian Geoffrey Blainey had used in a 1993 speech, and turbocharging it. In 1996, Howard rejected the view that Australia should apologise for its settler past:

> This 'black armband' view of our past reflects a belief that most Australian history since 1788 has been little more than a disgraceful story of imperialism, exploitation, racism, sexism and other forms of discrimination. I take a very different view. I believe that the balance sheet of our history is one of heroic achievement and that we have achieved much more as a nation of which we can be proud than of which we should be ashamed.[8]

Howard's 'different' view was the one that dominated Australia's culture. Formed by his middle class, white, methodist upbringing, Howard showed very little curiosity in the multitudinous ways of being human. You were either with him (and *like* him), and therefore deserving of grace, or against him, and subsequently should be mocked for your elitism and lack of sense.

The following decades were spent arguing over what 'version' of history should be taught in Australian schools. Teachers or lecturers who taught what happened to Indigenous people without absolving English settlers or those who came after them of any blame became targets. We are still feeling the effects of those 'history wars' today, with the school curriculum firmly in the firing line.

But while modern Australians could not be implicated in how settlers treated Indigenous people (that was in the past, and should be left there), they somehow drew credit from the Anzacs, whose actions were sacrosanct and needed to be remembered by – nay, imprinted on – every Australian, regardless of age. 'Today we join the past with the present; we confirm that that Anzac tradition permeates our modern life as it has permeated earlier generations,' he said in 2000, at the launch of the Gallipoli 2000 campaign.[9]

In Howard's history of Australia, we were the proud inheritors of past glories, and what we weren't proud of needn't be mentioned – perhaps hadn't even happened. After all, how can you be relaxed and comfortable if you're worried about things done in the past?

Paul Keating had his own foibles when it came to Australia's war history – in his view, Australia had been 'abandoned' by Britain during the Pacific campaigns of World War II and therefore should become a republic – but Howard stuck to 'tradition'. And that Howard-approved history is still the fallback of every Australian politician attempting to dog whistle at nationalism.

At the heart of this history was something called 'mateship', which Howard elevated to its current hallowed status. Indeed, he wanted to include the term in the preamble to the Constitution: 'Australians are free to be proud of their country and heritage, free to realise themselves as individuals, and free to pursue their hopes and ideals. We value excellence as well as fairness, independence as dearly as mateship', was his draft suggestion.[10] ('Free to be proud' is particularly telling.) You can't say he wasn't aware of optics – there was a reason he worked so hard to get Aden Ridgeway, then Australia's sole Indigenous parliamentarian, on board, under the guise of reaching across the political divide to the Democrats in the Senate.

Characteristically, 'mateship' was raised to a divisive end. Howard introduced the idea into the larger debate on whether Australia should hold a referendum on becoming a republic. The idea was to muddy the waters, and divide the 'yes' camp over an extraneous question. Howard only gave up on including mateship from the official referendum question after pushback from women and sections of the community not comfortable with the 'blokey' nature of the word. He pretended regret, having successfully distracted: 'I didn't want to give it up. I love the word. I think it's very evocative of something that means a lot to a lot of Australians.'[11] That 'something', of course, remained undefined – 'us' real Australians knew; 'those' women and the un-blokey would never get it.

Howard's rallying cry to enshrine mateship as one of the defining notions of Australian character was tied to his obsession with 'ordinary Australians'. Howard's 'battlers' were an evolution of Menzies's 'forgotten people', and decades later they morphed into Scott Morrison's 'quiet Australians'. Battlers understood mateship in a way the 'elites' never could. Progressives, city dwellers, 'chardonnay/soy latte sippers', intellectuals and those arguing for a reckoning of history were to be sneered at for their views, and could never, in Howard's telling, understand the sacred brotherhood of the ordinary Australian. Political correctness, which we would now refer to as 'woke', was certainly not an Australian value. Castigating the 'elites' was imported directly from the culture war playbook of the US Republican Party, and it worked. As political historian Judith Brett identified quite early, Howard shifted the core appeal of the Liberal Party from the idea it was the better economic manager, to the impression it was the stronger party of nationalism, moving its appeal from the boardroom to the suburbs, by speaking to these 'ordinary' universal traits of 'practical mateship'. Of course, Howard didn't invent the concept – the right has often used the ideas of bonds between (white) men as the unbreakable spirit that underpins 'ordinary' countrymen – but Honest John (a once ironic nickname because of his less than honest time as treasurer) made it the nation's personality.

So driven was Howard to push against any sort of 'elitism' he also included a swipe at his ideological enemies in his proposed Constitutional preamble: 'Australia's democratic and federal system of government exists under law to preserve and protect all Australians in an equal dignity which may never be infringed by prejudice or fashion or ideology nor invoked against achievement.' Or the short version – ideologies that went against Howard's Australia could be considered unconstitutional.

It didn't get as much attention as mateship, but it signalled the type of Australia Howard was hellbent on creating.

Under Howard, therefore, Anzac Day became holy. This was personal to Howard – his father and grandfather served in World War I – but he wasn't above cherry-picking other people's stories too. The last surviving veteran of Gallipoli, Alec Campbell, was a militant unionist and socialist who was known to have attended meetings of the Communist Party, but when Howard gave the eulogy at his funeral, he clipped off these inconvenient (even uncomfortable) protrusions and celebrated a one-eyed version of Campbell that better suited his Anzac myth-building.

Veneration for Anzac Day pre-dates Howard, but historian Martin Ball makes clear that as prime minister, Howard was at the 'vanguard' of the movement. If 'ordinariness' was coded nationalism, the Anzac myth was a useful push back against multiculturalism. As Ball points out, the 'Anzac is a myth of White Australia. It celebrates the nation as it was in 1915, when the white population reached a peak of 98 per cent.' As he wrote in 2004:

> The Anzac tradition holds many values for us all to celebrate, but the myth also suppresses parts of Australian history that are difficult to deal with. Anzac is a means of forgetting the origins of Australia. The Aboriginal population is conveniently absent. The convict stain is wiped clean. Postwar immigration is yet to broaden the cultural identity of the population.[12]

In the homogeneity of the Anzac myth, there was no need to worry about inclusion, or class, or acceptance, and therefore doing so was un-Anzac, un-mateship and un-Australian. You still see those arguments today – mateship and the 'fair go' trump identity politics (which is just being politically correct after all). So comprehensive has been the takeover of the national identity that the Australian War Memorial has received a half-a-billion-dollar makeover, while we struggle to comprehend our involvement in war crimes and people have been chased from the country and lost jobs for the crime of accurately describing the nation, and its history.

Equally, have you ever wondered why Australia Day is so polarising? In an impressive pincer movement,

Howard also elevated January 26 to a national loyalty test, taking it from a long weekend to a flashpoint in the culture wars. Under Keating, Australia had started to look at itself not purely from the point of view of its history and settlement, but from where it sat in the world. If Howard had been able to move Australia to the Atlantic, he would have. But instead he had to settle for moving Australia's culture back firmly into the Anglosphere.

Howard's campaign against reconciliation and the recognition of native title in the Mabo and Wik High Court decisions wasn't entirely symbolic – he passed actual legislation that gave pastoral and mining leases precedence over native title claims. But symbols were his genius and culture his battleground: weaponizing January 26 did more to harm multiculturalism than any legislation.

Thirteen years before his infamous 'we will decide who comes to this country and the circumstances in which they come' quote, Howard said that he didn't think it was 'wrong, racist, immoral or anything else for a country to say we will decide what the cultural identity and the cultural destiny of this country will be, and nobody else'.[13]

Ask anyone older than forty and they'll tell you about seeing the sudden shift in how Australia Day was celebrated, from a lazy end-of-summer long weekend that heralded the coming school and work year, to a jingoistic day with flags wrapped around cars and burnt shoulders – a day so sacred that moving a radio song countdown to a different date almost brought the nation to a halt. Before Howard, the flag and southern cross were largely reserved for sporting events (and even then people largely seemed to prefer the unofficial Boxing Kangaroo) and officialdom. It was almost embarrassing to be seen with the flag. After Howard, the Southern Cross tattoo became a signifier of a particular set of values, with 'love it or leave' the main mantra.

In 2023, Howard did admit the quiet part out loud, telling *The Australian*:

> I do hold the view that the luckiest thing that happened to this country was being colonised by the British. Not that they were perfect by any means, but they were infinitely more successful and beneficent colonisers than other European countries.[14]

And so the date upon which a British colony was formally established in New South Wales was the perfect pretext for an identity test (not that Howard would play identity politics, of course). If you celebrated the day, you were Australian. If you were ambivalent, you weren't, even if your ancestors had been here for 60,000 years rather than 200-odd. And if you were a more recent arrival hoping to add a bit of your own identity to the general mix, ideally you'd be excluded altogether. The citizenship test infamously asked who Australia's greatest ever cricketer was. Migrants had to answer questions about Don Bradman with a near-native level of English. The year before losing government, Howard made no apologies for the changes, saying:

> It would, however, be a crushing mistake to downplay the hopes and the expectations of our national family. We expect all who come here to make an overriding commitment to Australia, its laws and its democratic values. We expect them to master the common language of English and we will help them to do so.[15]

That's a far cry from the Australia he grew up in, where advertisements for workers for car factories proclaimed English was not necessary, but a reflection of his long-held discomfort with the concept of multiculturalism. And we all know what happens when Aussies are made to feel uncomfortable.

The answer: to commission a report. Shortly after coming to power, with Hanson steamrolling her way through what would become Howard's core constituency, Howard's government commissioned research into Australian attitudes on race for what was to be the basis of an 'anti-racism education program'. The subsequent report was kept secret, until Emeritus Professor of Sociology Andrew Jakubowicz's persistence led to its eventual release.[16] It found that the Hansonite rhetoric was creating a 'crisis' in what it meant to be Australian and there was 'a clear need for an anti-racism campaign'.

But the Howard government refused to adopt the most obvious tool to hand, the UN's International Day for the Elimination of Racial Discrimination. Instead, on the very same date, they installed 'Harmony Day' – 'a celebration of cultural diversity'. After all, if Australia was to sign up to a day that called for eliminating racism, it would have to acknowledge racism existed, and that was not part of Howard's culture plan for the nation.

Unsurprisingly, the harmless Harmony Day passes most of us by unnoticed, and Australia still cannot reckon with its racism. ABC senior journalist Laura Tingle found herself at the centre of a right-wing firestorm in 2024, when she made the reasonable comment that Australia was a racist country. Tingle was responding to the contention in parliament of then–opposition leader, Peter Dutton, that migrants were responsible for Australia's housing crisis (but not in the racist way, you understand, just in the common sense, 'you're picking up what I am putting down', non-racist way, obviously). Dutton was never subtle with his dog whistling, but by the time he was leading the Liberal Party he didn't need to be. Both Australia, and the party he directed, had changed enough that pointing out obvious prejudices was more offensive than the prejudices themselves.

That shift, too, we can lay at Howard's feet.

Academic Carol Johnson identified it in her 2000 book, *Governing Change: Keating to Howard*, writing:

> There was no need to reconstruct Australian identity; white, heterosexual, Anglo-Celtic males could once again rest assured in their central role in Australian political culture. Australia was not an Asian country. White Australians could be proud of their history of achievement despite 'blemishes'. People could be 'relaxed and comfortable'.[17]

And even today, relaxed and comfortable are not only encouraged, they are actively pursued by both major political parties. Not everyone can be relaxed and comfortable – only those who don't see the need for any changes can claim that particular prize. It's one of Howard's greatest legacies, won through dividing and distracting us with seemingly never-ending culture wars.

Much like becoming a republic or changing the flag, the date January 26 became so intertwined with white notions of 'Australianess' that any council that chooses NOT to acknowledge it through a citizenship ceremony faces a public inquisition.

As recently as 2025, there was a private member's bill in front of the parliament to enshrine the date as Australia Day in legislation. Never mind that for decades the date for the public holiday moved around (depending on the state or whether the Friday or the Monday was closest), or that it caused obvious pain to Indigenous Australians, or that until Howard made it a big deal, most Australians didn't appear particularly attached to the day or even knew what it commemorated, it is now a sacred date and there can be no other date used to represent Australia's day.

Howard thrived leading culture wars, and in 2006 he felt comfortable enough to say that 'the divisive, phony debate about national identity and what it means for our influence in the world has been finally laid to rest', while listing his achievements across a decade in power. The nation has yet to recover, and all because no one ever managed to convince Howard that what he believed was right wasn't right for everyone, let alone the country.

Having established Australia as holding the values of an 'ordinary' white man, Howard turned his attention to keeping Australia 'straight'.

In 2004, his government (with support from the Labor opposition) passed legislation that defined 'marriage' under Australian law for the first time. That definition meant the legal union was 'between a man and a woman'. Twenty years later, he explained: 'We put it in there because we knew if we left it unsaid some judge somewhere in Australia would say, "I think a marriage is between a man and a man or a woman and a woman".'[18] This anxiety about judicial law-making was another line of attack Howard imported from the US. (For someone who was so grateful Australia was colonised by the

British, Howard did a remarkable amount to re-colonise the country in America's image.) Howard himself remained a central figure in the 'traditional' corner during the 2017 plebiscite debate, where he urged his party and the electorate to vote against marriage equality.

And his anti-gay position wasn't confined to marriage. In 2004 he said:

> I'm against gay adoption, just as I'm against gay marriage. I think there are certain benchmark institutions and arrangements in our society that you don't muck around with. Children ideally should be brought up by a mother and a father who are married. That's the ideal.[19]

A ban on gay couples adopting children from overseas was floated, but Howard ran out of time to implement it before the 2007 election.

He may have lost that battle (in the 2017 plebiscite the Australian community overwhelmingly declared itself comfortable with gay marriage), but the war wages on. Now it's transgender people that have become the main target. By the simple expedient of nominating an 'ideal' – again, one drawn from the past rather than the present, let alone the future – Howard divided us into those who lived ideally and those who did not.

*

Howard didn't invent culture wars, but he did master the art of not just fighting them, dividing his opponents *and* winning votes while he was at it. His successors have leveraged his lessons in various, depressing ways, albeit with varying degrees of sophistication and success.

Abbott led the country as close to what he imagined Howard wanted as possible, but never quite mastered Howard's practised 'averageness' that helped sell it. Morrison did his best to call back to Howard's battlers, but couldn't uphold the facade he was one of the 'quiet Australians'. Dutton ramped up the 'us and them' mantra, but only ever knew how to play one note on the dog whistle trumpet and never knew how to hit it softly. But each of them managed to forward one or more of Howard's culture wars to the point many can't recognise a time before they existed. Australia has shifted in the years since Howard's vision ruled supreme, but it has never seen an equal correction to the division he created. For the record, conservative commentator Gerard Henderson believed Howard failed in the culture wars, because he didn't manage to completely grind the ABC into the dust. But Howard's success is evident in our circular national debates, the well-worn battle lines and the constant callback to an Australia that never truly existed.

Howard's success lay not only in his conviction that he was right and his unwavering belief his values needed to become the nation's, but also in his consistency. He has rarely taken a backward step, as he told Speers and other journalists in 2006, and if he has ever developed reservations about the positions he has taken (and continues to take), he's certainly kept it to himself.

Ultimately, he set the battlefield and the terms in which culture wars are to be fought, boundaries that still hold today. His skill, which remains unrivalled in modern Australian politics, was picking the issues he wanted to blow up at exactly the right time that would unite his base while enraging his opponents and persuading the middle. And the failures of his successors to convince the electorate for very long highlight one of Howard's central features: his ability to be both authentic and manipulative simultaneously. That too makes sense – facsimiles lose quality the further they are from the original. Howard was playing a role, but that role was John Howard. Abbott, Morrison, Dutton tried playing Howard as well, and failed.

Howard's cultural framing continues to booby-trap the public debate. We've not been able to shake the sense that 'ordinary' Australians are stuck in the past and politics has been on the defensive ever since (and supporters of the Voice referendum have the scars to prove it). Labor supporters will still tell you the Albanese government cannot change too much because of what the 'conservatives will do'. This is despite the conservatives having gone backwards for two elections in a row and, as of the most recent election (2025), holding a historically low representation in the House of Representatives.

It doesn't matter that legacy media, which perpetuates the Howard framing of political debate, is failing to win new audiences – if Labor doesn't toe the line, we could have [enter name here] (who knows who the leader of the Liberal Party is currently, or if it still exists by the time you are reading this) as prime minister if it's not careful! That attitude, right there, is the enduring power of John Howard.

2

Housing

'Anybody who owns a house is very happy that the value of that house has gone up, let's be quite straight about that. I haven't found anybody in seven and a half years shake their fist at me and say, "I'm angry with you for letting the value of my house increase". So it's not a problem if you own a house. It's true that to get into the market in the first place it's harder if the prices continue going up. But, of course, the interest rates now are much lower than they were seven and a half years ago, about $430 a month on average around Australia [. . .] And one of the reasons why housing prices have gone up is that people can afford to borrow more because interest rates are lower. In a sense, we are the victims of our own success and our own prosperity.'[1]

John Howard, September 2003

The roots of Australia's current housing unaffordability crisis can be traced back to the Howard government's housing policies, which turbocharged investment in a way never seen before in this country: thanks to them (and successive governments who have done absolutely nothing to wind back the changes, or even help even out the playing field), the great Australian dream of homeownership is increasingly a fantasy. Or, if you have stretched yourself thin to just break into the market, a nightmare.

In this 2003 talkback radio session on ABC Brisbane, Howard celebrated the worker's paradise he'd created, and the ensuing higher house prices. 'I mean, what Australian employees have experienced over the last few years is, in a sense, the treble,' he told the presenter, Steve Austin (who was renting at the time).

> They've had lower interest rates, they've higher real wages and they've had job security and more jobs. Now you add those three together and people naturally feel they can take on more obligations, that's human nature.
>
> Now I ask people to not take on obligations they can't service and there are always some people who overreach and there's always some danger in relation to those people. But let's not be frightened of stability and prosperity.

Here are many of the Howard hallmarks: describing what's happening as completely 'natural', anyone not prospering as foolish (for 'overreach'), and patronising the counterview as ridiculous. But people weren't 'frightened of stability': they were experiencing radical, almost rabid, change. The International Monetary Fund had just released a clear and rather shocking graph about Australian housing prices:

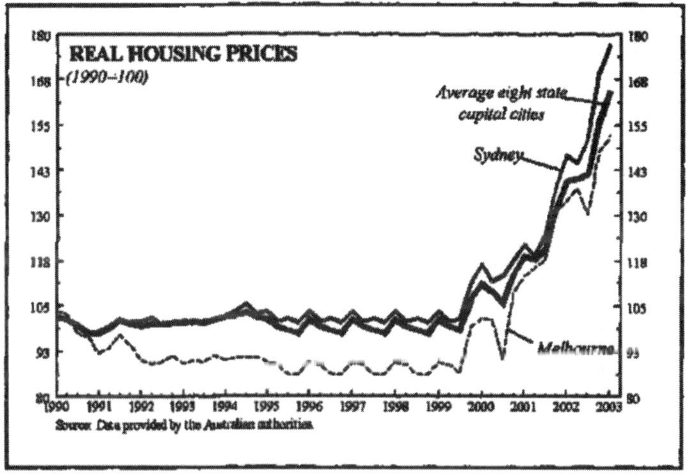

Source: International Monetary Fund, Australia, Staff Report for the 2003 Article IV Consultation, September 3, 2003

And their report contained the explanation Howard was trying to cover up: by the end of 2002, investor housing accounted for 30 per cent of the stock of housing loans, compared to 18 per cent a decade ago.[2]

In fact, one of the ABC Brisbane callers who rang in to speak to Howard that day DID want to complain about the increase in her home's value.[3] Phyllis pointed out something obvious: that higher house prices didn't make you richer if you still needed to live in a house:

> I won't be as aggressive as to shake my fist at you, but I'll certainly shake my finger at you when you say that someone who owns their home has no problem, they're sitting on a nice little nest egg. We're on a pension and we would like to sell our homes, go into a unit or a townhouse or something. But we can't do that because if we do, we're going to spend the whole amount just on a townhouse or a unit and we'll have nothing left over if we need to do anything to it. So we're stuck.

Howard disagreed with her, and he used his time-honoured tactic of semantics to do it.

'Look Phyllis, what I said was that not everybody was sitting on a nest egg. I said people had not complained about the value of their house going up.'

Phyllis was adamant she wanted to be the first one: 'I've broken the mould.'

But what she underestimated was that Howard understood how she felt better than she did herself. Howard couldn't be wrong if you were wrong about how you actually felt.

'Well, you're not . . . you're not actually complaining,' Howard said, warming up to reframe Phyllis's concerns in real time, just in case any listeners were confused as to what was going on. 'What you're really saying is the value of a house hasn't gone up enough.'

Phyllis tried. She really did.

'No, no, no. I disagree. I think that it is ridiculous that the inflation of the housing prices . . . what about our grandchildren?'

Dear reader, WE are Phyllis's grandchildren, so let's listen carefully to Howard's justification for why we can't afford a house.

'I'm not saying that there aren't problems for people buying for the first time, but you have to look at it in terms of both existing homeowners and future homeowners and what we have to try and do, and you quite rightly identify in relation to your grandchildren, is to find ways of mitigating the cost of getting into your first home.

'But we can't and shouldn't do that at the cost of reducing the wealth effect and the wealth value of people who have existing properties, there's nothing to be gained by that. We have to find some other ways of ameliorating the cost of buying your first home.'

So the problem is not that houses get more and more expensive, it's that first home buyers don't have enough money. And did we ever find 'some other ways of ameliorating the cost of buying your first home'? Reader, we did not.

Phyllis tried one more time, arguing about the need for one of Howard's favourite values, 'common sense'.

'You know, it's ridiculous. I mean, you're not seeing value in the $500,000 you're spending on some broken down old dump and . . . that's where we are at the moment,' Phyllis tried for the final time.

She stood no chance.

Instead, we had the parable of Honest John (and his wife, Janette), who were Just Like Everyone Else.

'The only substantial asset I have along with my wife is my home.

'And that's a very important asset to me and I think I'm typical of most Australians in saying that and the fact that the value of our principal asset has risen is due in no small measures to the fact that we now have very low interest rates and people can afford therefore to buy more.

'Now I wouldn't like, and I don't think you'd like, and I don't think your grandchildren would like, interest rates to go up. If interest rates went up sharply, that will certainly have an effect on house prices over time, but it would also have an adverse effect on the rest of the economy . . . there's nothing to be gained by that.'

It might not be obvious now, but the spectre of rising interest rates was a mini-scare campaign all by itself. Howard was invoking the 17 per cent interest rate peak during 1990. The memory was fresh enough that just mentioning 'rising interest rates' was enough to get people shuddering and counting their good fortune that they were already in the housing market, and if they weren't, well, they'd get there. After all, it was tough for their parents too, right? And, as always, there was nothing to be gained by doing things differently.

Ultimately, as we know, Phyllis was right to worry about her grandchildren's generation in the face of Howard's self-satisfaction. It doesn't take an economics degree to work out what happened, just a brief description of what housing meant before this, which Phyllis no doubt remembered.

After World War II, housing was a foundation of the postwar reconstruction plan created and implemented by former Labor prime ministers John Curtin and Ben Chifley and Director-General of Postwar Reconstruction Herbert Cole 'Nugget' Coombs. It not only eliminated slums and gave returning soldiers and a nation indebted to them a chance to get back on their feet by ensuring a roof over their heads, it also created long term employment. Housing, then, meant a safe and secure place to live – some people owned property, many had the government as their landlord – the point was that people were guaranteed a lifelong home.

Then Robert Menzies came along in the 1950s and brought along the conservative idea of homeownership. He believed it gave people a tangible stake in the community they lived in, as well as something they could *conserve* and hand down to their own families. We know this because Menzies told us. In a 1949 election speech, he laid bare his intent to 'aid' 'little Capitalists' to own their own home.[4] This was an attack on a Labor politician who had said that Labor was focused on ensuring workers had a home, not with making workers 'little Capitalists'.[5] Menzies seized on the line and used it as the first step in changing attitudes about housing from a necessity and public good to an asset that accrued value and increased individual wealth.

Menzies's attitude slowly took over as the dominant one, and thanks to his government's programs that allowed housing tenants to purchase their government home (often discounted), homeownership rates increased from 53 per cent in 1947 to 73 per cent in 1966. Strikingly, the 2021 census shows homeownership rates in Australia now sit at around 66 per cent. And while we could all sit around scratching our heads wondering who did this, the data is pretty clear.

It was Howard.

Howard turned housing from a place to live to a source of wealth. It went from a roof over your head to a way to build an investment portfolio. He essentially supercharged Menzies' idea of 'little Capitalists' and created 'little property developers', where the great Australian dream of owning your own home became owning your own investment property. The Commonwealth Bank even created an advertising campaign on how to get your own investment property loan. Now, we are at the mercy of property speculators who gamble on property prices continuing to increase. Data obtained by the ABC from the Australian Tax Office in 2024 showed 2500 property investors owned 33,200 rentals between them.[6] They don't even need to risk their own money – with the way the banking system is geared, they are able to leverage their existing property equity to roll into the next investment.

They can do that because of the tax breaks from 'negative gearing', which provides the tax cover for owning an investment, essentially enabling an investor making a loss on property costs (including interest payments) to deduct this loss from their tax – in effect a government subsidy for their loan.

Negative gearing for housing investment has existed in some form since 1936 when the Lyons government introduced it to boost housing supply during the Great Depression (other than for a short interlude when the Hawke government abolished and then reinstated it).

Negative gearing (although not ideal) isn't an issue by itself, but in 1999/2000, Howard and his treasurer, Peter Costello, decided to overhaul the tax system to 'encourage investment'. Fifteen years before, in 1985, Hawke and Keating had introduced a capital gains tax – that is, a tax on the profit you made from an investment. Howard had always hated it and spent the next couple of elections campaigning against it, but by the 1996 election, it had become a permanent part of the tax system. So in a very Howard move, he sought to hollow it out instead of scrapping it, through the guise of 'reform': he introduced a capital gains discount of 50 per cent for investments held for more than twelve months.

If we wanted to be generous to Howard, we could say it was not his *intention* to set the housing market ablaze – affordable property became the unintended sacrifice of Howard's war against the capital gains tax. But the effect is clear. If you look at the housing price graph those noted Communists at the International Monetary Fund provided in 2003, you should be able to see what that did to property prices.

The capital gains reform is a very early example of Howard's ideological outlook leading to negative outcomes for the nation – and while he may not have intended for home prices to rise (and continue rising and rising), he did nothing to counter its impact. Presumably there was 'nothing to be gained'.

Let's say we bought one of the rundown shacks Phyllis was complaining about for $500,000, held on to it for a couple of years and then sold it for a million. We've made half a million in profit, but we will only pay tax on $250,000.

As investments go, it's as safe as houses – as long as the property market continues to increase. It's those hoping to get into the housing market who are paying the price. In 1999, the median house price in Sydney was $272,500. By 2003 it had increased to $454,250. In 2025, it was $1.7 million and still rising.[8]

Combine the existing negative gearing policy with the capital gains discount and you have minimised tax on both sides of the tax coin. Keep the property (or properties) to minimise your tax while owning it, and then when the market hits a sweet spot, sell, and half the profit is tax free. Rinse and repeat.

And those who can afford it, do. The richest 10 per cent of Australians receive 82 per cent of the total benefits of the capital gains discount.[9] In 2025, negative gearing cost the Budget $7.4 billion and the capital gains tax discount for residential property accounted for $6 billion. That's $13.4 billion in lost revenue, and looking at the data a little more, that means the top 10 per cent of earners received $7.5 billion in tax incentives, as a reward for increasing the median housing price by about 400 per cent over the last twenty-five years.

This is not new information. In fact, around the same time Phyllis was calling up ABC Brisbane to let Howard know of her concern for property prices in the future, the government itself was having a small 'oh dear' moment and had the Productivity Commission check in on what was going on with housing.

Cabinet documents from 2004, released on New Year's Day in 2025, showed that the alarm bells were already ringing over the capital gains tax (CGT) change and what it had done to the housing market. As the *Sydney Morning Herald* reported, the Productivity Commission had noted negative gearing and the CGT concession had 'combined to magnify the attractiveness of investing in residential property during the recent upswing in house prices, thereby adding to price pressures.'[10]

The Productivity Commission weren't being alarmist. In between 2002 and 2004, prices had increased by more than 40 per cent in Sydney, nearly 65 per cent in Brisbane, where Phyllis was calling from, and almost 30 per cent in Melbourne.

Tax data also shows how investment was driving this demand. In the year before the Howard government, CGT concessional changes came into play, landlords reported a net profit of $156 million in 1999–2000. In 2002–03, there was a reported net rental loss of $1.5 billion. That figure doubled in 2003–04 and peaked at a record $9.1 billion in 2007–08. Residential landlords only reported a net gain when interest rates were held at almost zero by the Reserve Bank during the Covid pandemic, but the increases will soon see it return to the pattern of billions of dollars in losses set by the Howard era.

Howard was worried about property prices swinging the *other* way and what that would mean politically, in terms of support from his 'battlers', and so they didn't act.

And neither has any other government since, mostly for the same reasons.

To its credit, the Labor oppositions of 2016 and 2019 did attempt to put investment tax reform on the national agenda. Its 2016 attempt was mostly forgotten in the shock result that saw Labor give a real scare to the Malcolm Turnbull-led Coalition. In 2019, frightened by the upcoming generational shift that could have made tax reform a welcome reality, Labor was hit with a scare campaign so effective it killed off any attempts at political bravery for the following half decade. Which is another hangover from Howard – he's still dictating how his political rivals react as well. Looking at the electoral data from 2019, the top ten richest electorates in Australia, the ones who would be impacted the most by Labor's proposed tax reforms, voted FOR Labor. It was the bottom ten, the actual battlers, who swung against Labor. Howard's knack of having people vote against their own economic interest has been passed down the party line.

Remember Howard's idea that rather than keeping housing affordable, all that was needed was 'ameliorating' the position of the buyer trying to enter the market? He tried it, bringing back the first homeowner grants the Hawke government had previously scrapped. In July 2000, the grant was $7000. In 2001, it was increased to $14,000 for those building new homes (as part of a response to the uncertainty following the September 11 attacks), wound back to $7000 by June 2002. Then came the 2008 Global Financial Crisis and the Rudd government borrowed from the Howard playbook and expanded the grants to $14,000 for existing homes and $21,000 for new homes. They were eventually wound back to $7000 by 2010 and then scrapped entirely in 2012.

So not only did these grants not 'ameliorate' the position of first home buyers, they made it worse. Research looking at the impacts of the grants found they added about $57,000 to the median home, which was $360,000 at the time. And notice that the grants came along every time there looked to be a slump in the housing market: house prices have never had an opportunity to correct in Australia, because after Howard governments have consistently intervened to keep them inflated whenever the market did start to dip.

Naturally most governments, including Howard's, have blamed other forces, notably supply, and, more recently, immigration (we'll get to immigration . . .). But again, the numbers tell a different story. Between 2015 and 2025, the population increased by 16 per cent. Over that same period, the number of dwellings increased by 19 per cent. During that same period, the median house price increased by 61 per cent – twice the inflation rate (which was 33 per cent as measured by CPI). And if supply was the main issue, you would expect to see (or so most economists would tell you) rents increase at about the same rate as house prices. But we haven't. Between 2015 and 2025, rents have increased by 24 per cent. Lower than the general rate of inflation (with the main driver coming in the last three years when rents really started to jump as people, fatigued from Covid lockdowns, sought out properties of their own, rather than sharing – which lower- and middle-income earners have felt the most).

In case anyone thinks the last decade has been some sort of fluke: house prices have increased fivefold between 2000 and 2025, while inflation has increased 103 per cent. Rents largely matched the inflation figures, coming in at 115 per cent (again, it's the people who can least afford it who usually find themselves priced out first, even with rents). If supply was the issue, or migrants were filling up every home, then rents would rise like purchase prices, and it simply isn't the case.

So, what has been the result?

Well, a generation that has been left completely screwed and largely at the mercy of the 'Bank of Mum and Dad', the ultimate 'amelioration' of circumstance. Unlike those parents, who took on loans about three times their annual salary, home buyers entering the market are looking at a loan at least eight times their yearly income.[11] If you are lucky enough to have parents who can afford it, homeownership is still within your grasp. Otherwise, it's a nightmare in an increasingly insecure post-Covid rental market. People are buying later, with loan periods that extend well into their retirement, meaning they need to use their super to pay off the loan. And if you still have housing costs at retirement in Australia, you are looking at a very bleak future. The pension is not enough to cover the average rent, or mortgage payment, let alone anything else. Howard's Australia firmly entrenched generational wealth – you've either got it, or you don't.

And if you don't, well, that's somehow your fault for buying avocado toast and not at all the fault of the tax and policy settings that have been set against you and then never changed because the person who introduced them created a war between the present and the future, with all the fire-power given to the present (and increasingly the past). Phyllis had the sense to worry about her grandchildren. Howard sold them down the river. The scare campaign continued to work two decades on.

What's really scary, though, is the consequence of this war against the future. Those who have come after realise that they've been sold a lie. It doesn't matter that they have done everything right – getting educated, getting the stable job, saving. Combine the lack of housing affordability with stagnant wages and an almost impossible task of getting ahead, and not only do you get generations furious at the betrayal, but you also get lower birth rates. (And what do you know, as of late 2025, there were already calls to reintroduce the Howard era 'baby bonus', another absurd 'amelioration'.) The natural conclusion to Howard's war on the future is no grandchildren at all.

3
Race

> 'I do not accept that there is underlying racism in this country. I have always taken a more optimistic view of the character of the Australian people. I do not believe Australians are racist.'[1]
>
> John Howard, December 2005

You have probably heard of the dog whistle (political speak for coded language), where the intended recipients hear something others may not. It's most famous for allowing politicians to be racist, without having to ever say the quiet parts out loud. Those who are primed to hear the messages do, but for everyone else the politician has a 'plausible' deniability.

By the time he was prime minister, Howard didn't have a dog whistle, he had a whole canine trumpet. One of his greatest skills was knowing what notes to play – and how hard to blow.

A good number of Australians had indeed been primed, feeling sidelined, scared or outright hostile at the Australia that Paul Keating had been dragging the nation towards, in which Indigenous and immigrant Australians were more accepted, a republic was a possibility and our geographical place as an Asian nation was recognised as a reality. Howard played to white picket fences. As early as 1988, when he was Leader of the Opposition, he concocted a 'One Australia' policy – a title he insisted on as a riposte to the term 'multiculturalism', believing there should only be 'one' Australian culture. He was still promoting the term as late as 2007 (long after you would have thought its similarity with 'One Nation' would have revealed it as the dog whistle it was): 'I have always believed in One Australia. I believe in that passionately. It's influenced my views in relation to multiculturalism, to settlement policies. I have always supported a multi-racial mix in this country, but I have always believed that we should be one nation, one people.'[2] So I guess it's okay to look a bit different, as long as you think and behave exactly the same.

It's not too much of a stretch to take Howard at his word that he had 'always believed' there should only be 'one' Australian nation and people. His father, Lyall Howard, was described in a 1989 profile written by journalist Milton Cockburn as a 'proud patriot', adding 'there are family suspicions he was a member of the New Guard, the unofficial militia which prospered between the wars'.[3]

What was the New Guard? It was a fascist movement that for a short moment flourished in New South Wales during the Great Depression (from 1931–35), and, according to its membership application form, stood for:

- unswerving loyalty to the throne
- all for the British Empire
- sane and honourable government throughout Australia
- suppression of any disloyal and immoral elements in government, industrial and social circles
- abolition of machine politics
- maintenance of the full liberty of the individual.[4]

Sound familiar?

While it is only speculated (including by his son, Bob) that Lyall was a New Guardsman, it is undisputed that he was very conservative. Those views, compounded by the conservatism of Howard's mother and the church he grew up in, have remained evident in Howard's approach to race – and his refusal to see how it matters – his entire life. Howard has willingly remained stuck in his view of the 1950s, one which, in his white, middle-class neighbourhood of Earlwood at least, appeared equal and rewarded hard work. Bob Howard, in Marion Maddox's *God Under Howard: The rise of the religious right in Australian politics*, summed it up as '[Our] family had a real us-and-them thing. It was the climate we grew up in, not at all modified by the church.'[5]

Cultural expert and associate professor Fiona Allon wrote in her 2008 book, *Renovation Nation*:

> [. . .] the cherished symbols of Howard's world reveal a process of selective memory and idealisation. His sporting hero, Don Bradman, doesn't simply represent the game of cricket, but a particular tradition of cricket associated with white, middle-class Protestant men, free of any trace of the sectarianism that the history of cricket in Australia possesses. The heroics of Gallipoli and the 'spirit of Anzac', the image of the Aussie battler, the values of mateship and egalitarian innocence, are fictions in exactly the same way, belonging to and drawn from a fictional, idealised past. That they were fictions didn't make them any less effective as political tools, however.[6]

Not just tools but guiding principles, and the blueprint to how he wanted to shape Australia to look. Malcolm Fraser, who had at one point flirted with the idea of Howard becoming his successor ahead of the ambitious Andrew Peacock, eventually turned on Howard before his 1983 election loss. Fraser said it came down to Howard's views of race, as Howard was the lone minister in his government to speak against allowing

Vietnamese refugees into Australia and had also stood against applying trade sanctions on the apartheid South African government.

In an early example of how Howard would conflate the moral position with the one he most fervently believed in, in 1975 he said the only way to defeat apartheid was . . . to do nothing, claiming that was the most ethical position.

> If we are ever going to achieve a situation in which the horrible racial discrimination which does occur in South Africa and which is probably a level of racial discrimination which is duplicated in many countries throughout the world is ever going to be broken down we are not going to break it down by hermetically sealing off South Africa from the rest of the world, we are not going to break it down by having no contact with the South Africans and we are certainly not going to break it down by preventing cricket contests between South Africa and Australia.[7]

That is, incidentally, exactly how it *was* broken.

It was still too early in 1988 to be as overt as Howard was in questioning multiculturalism and the Liberal Party had not yet developed into the hive mind it later became following his final leadership stint, which meant there was still plenty of debate about policy direction, no matter who the leader was. His policy platform,

'One Australia', along with his comments questioning Asian migration, gave Labor what it needed to paint the Liberals and Howard as wanting a return to a discriminatory migration policy, and Howard was back in the political cold, losing the election and the leadership of the party. Most politicians would give up at this point. Not Howard.

But it was only short term. John Hewson, a former advisor to Howard, lost the 'unlosable' 1993 election, and a bumbling Alexander Downer had the Liberals turning back to the last man standing – Howard. He had learnt his lesson: don't be too loud – but give people permission to be uncomfortable. Not just uncomfortable – hostile.

To do this, Howard helped stoke fears – completely unfounded then, and now – that recent High Court decisions in Mabo and Wik would mean Indigenous Australians could 'come and claim your backyard'. He had spent years framing push back against racist scaremongering as mere 'political correctness' and by the mid-1990s, with Paul Keating on the nose, increasing economic insecurity and an uneasy white population fearing the uncertainty of reform, Howard's insistence Australians had a right to be 'relaxed and comfortable' was a heady temptation.

Howard's 'One Australia' attitudes might have had to be rebranded but they had not changed. In 1989, Howard told political commentator Gerard Henderson:

> The objection I have to multiculturalism is that multiculturalism is in effect saying that it is impossible to have an Australian ethos, that it is impossible to have a common Australian culture. So we have to pretend that we are a federation of cultures and that we've got a bit from every part of the world. I think that is hopeless.[8]

Even in 1996, he still couldn't say the quiet part out loud – but as it turned out, he didn't need to. Along came the Oxley Liberal candidate, Pauline Hanson.

Hanson was loud, brash, and, most importantly, *ordinary.* She hadn't got the memo about turning down the volume on One Australia, and was therefore booted from the Liberal Party before the 1996 election. She ran as an independent, romped into power, shocked and titillated with her maiden speech that warned Australia was being 'swamped by Asians' and then spent the next few years enthralling the media class, who elevated her to a cult-like unstoppable force. Hanson WAS Howard's Australia, so in a speech to the Queensland Liberal Party – delivered twelve days after Hanson's maiden parliamentary speech – Howard gave his tacit approval to her racist provocations:

> One of the great changes that have come over Australia in the last six months is that people do feel able to speak a little more freely and a little

> more openly about what they feel. In a sense the pall of censorship on certain issues has been lifted. I think we were facing the possibility of becoming a more narrow and restrictive society and that free speech could not be taken so easily for granted as we might in our calmer moments have assumed. I think there has been that change and I think that's a very good thing. And I hope it continues but like everything a right such as free speech carries with it responsibilities and I welcome the fact that people can now talk about certain things without living in fear of being branded as a bigot or as a racist or any of the other expressions that have been too carelessly flung around in this country whenever somebody has disagreed with what somebody has said.[9]

By late 1997, Hanson was a political celebrity, dominating the culture. The more her views, speech and ignorance was mocked, the stronger she grew. In the absence of political pushback from Howard, former prime minister Bob Hawke attempted to have his predecessors and successors come together in a show of unity condemning Hanson and her views. Hawke, Paul Keating and Gough Whitlam co-signed a statement denouncing Hanson.

Malcolm Fraser declined to sign because he was hoping to gather his own party to sign their own equivalent statement, but he had publicly agreed with the sentiments of his political rivals.

Howard declined to take part, claiming he did not wish to 'elevate' the views of an independent backbencher. That and he was too busy letting Hanson broaden the boundaries of 'acceptable' speech, which he then capitalised on.

There has been a lot of rewriting history when it comes to Howard's treatment of One Nation. Most people over forty will have some memory of his decree that there were to be no preference deals with the party, and those not paying attention have taken that to mean he stood against Hanson. Howard only pushed back against Hanson following the 1998 Queensland election when it became obvious that she was cannibalising the Liberal Party vote. And so, Howard started working in earnest to bring her voters back under his tent.

The modern rise of the far right can be traced back to John Howard's embrace of Hansonisms within the Liberal Party. She is, and remains to be, a useful tool for those of Howard's ilk to condone racist attitudes without ever having to speak the words themselves. But such is the shift that it takes extreme speech for politicians to react – as happened when Fraser Anning, elected to the Senate on a One Nation ticket, used the phrase 'final solution' when discussing Muslim immigration in 2018.

Hanson has been so useful to Howard's Liberal Party that following her re-election to the Senate in 2016 after a period in the (shall we say) political wilderness that included jail, convictions expunged, deregistration of her political party, a stint on reality TV, threats to move to England, and then rehabilitation via breakfast television and eventual return to the parliament, Howard urged his party to embrace her, both for her votes in the senate and her voter base. They did, defending her right to be a bigot when she wore a burqa in the Senate as part of a xenophobic stunt, and, following Howard's 1996 example, largely ignored her claims that Australia was being 'swamped by Muslims' (a claim as untrue as her statement that Australia was being 'swamped by Asians').

The 'One Australia' sentiment wasn't idle in Hanson's absence, however: by the time of her return, Australian politics was well-conditioned to Islamophobia and the 'othering' of various groups of people. Even by 2001 there was more than enough social licence for the 'Pacific Solution', a policy where asylum seekers were not only denied legal rights to apply for asylum, but forced into mandatory offshore detention. It's a treatment so harsh Donald Trump looks at it admiringly as something to emulate, but it's considered so normal to Australians now that the Labor government can reopen offshore detention centres in Nauru with a billion-dollar price tag and receive barely an eyebrow raise in response.

The terrorist attacks of September 11, 2001, helped: Howard was able to start pushing his views and 'values' a little louder, in the name of Australia's 'security'. Racism could be centre stage in Australia again, just as long as it wasn't completely overt. In 2004, Howard was forced to condemn a 2000 photo of Australian soldiers wearing Ku Klux Klan–style hoods posing with black recruits ahead of a deployment.[10] But in a sign of just how much Australia had already shifted, then local Liberal MP for Townsville, Peter Lindsay, defended the soldiers' actions as a 'fun thing before the troops went overseas', denying there was a need for any further inquiry.

Just in case you thought there might be consequences for someone condoning what Howard himself condemned, fear not. Howard promoted Lindsay to assistant minister for defence three years later.

Anti-Muslim sentiment grew in Australia under Howard, reaching a crescendo in the Cronulla race riots of December 2005, in which 5000 mostly white Australians gathered on a Sydney beach to 'take back' the area from 'outsiders'. Thousands of text messages had flown around Sydney urging Aussies to come and support 'Leb and wog bashing day', pushed on by elements of the media – including Howard's favourite Alan Jones – and resulted in white men draped in the Australian flag, bearing signs declaring 'we grew here you flew here', attacking anyone they believed to be Muslim or Middle Eastern.[11] Howard, though, couldn't see the racism. 'I do not accept that there is underlying racism in this country,' he said in response to the attack.

'I have always taken a more optimistic view of the character of the Australian people. I do not believe Australians are racist.'[12]

Not only that, Howard didn't want anyone 'rushing to judgement' over what was at the heart of the riots and attacks (spoiler: it was racism) and instead wanted everyone to chill and remember all those Australian values he had spent the better part of a decade reframing as the nation's personality while also engaging in a bit of victim blaming, lest anyone start to feel a little less relaxed and comfortable about who was really at fault here. A day after the riot, Howard said:

> But overwhelmingly the desire of the Australian community is to have a nation which is united behind all of those values and in a nation that wants nothing other than a full commitment to this country's future from all people, irrespective of their background. It means of course that newcomers to this country must embrace our values. It means that those who were born here must respect and accept as fellow Australians, those who have chosen to make this country their home.
>
> Now those things may sound as a statement of the obvious. But I think sometimes on occasions like this it is a good idea to state the obvious because sometimes it is lost sight of. And the most obvious thing about yesterday is that the law was broken

> and people who break the law should be punished. And if the law was broken last weekend when lifesavers were bashed [the preceding event which was used as the catalyst to gather 'Aussies' to 'take back the beach'] then those people should be punished as well. And first and foremost, this does involve a challenge to the maintenance of law and order. I don't think we should begin to categorise it at this stage as anything other than that.[13]

So it was a law-and-order issue, nothing to do with race – except to the extent people with different 'values' aren't welcome. The leader of the country sets the tone on how the majority should react to events, and Howard's tone was one of 'tsk, tsk law breakers', but also, 'victims, have you considered just becoming Australian?'

In an interview the following year, in response to criticism from Muslim leaders concerned over comments Howard had made about Muslim values and their treatment of women, Howard again blew the 'values' note on his trumpet:

> I've said generally of migrants who come to this country, no matter where they've come from, they have to integrate.
>
> That means speaking English as quickly as possible, it means embracing Australian values, and

> it also means making sure that no matter what the culture of the country from which they came might have been, Australia requires women to be treated fairly and decently and in the same fashion as men.
>
> If any migrants coming to this country have a different view, they'd better get rid of that view pretty quickly.
>
> Ninety-nine per cent of the Islamic community of Australia has integrated and is part of the Australian community, but I've said before there is a small section – and that's self-evident – that is unwilling to integrate, and it's up to all of us to try and overcome that resistance.[14]

Howard knew of the power of the 'good migrant' trope, which allowed people uncomfortable with other cultures or races to claim it wasn't an issue of racism that drove them, but 'values'. And instead of gender equality, in 2006 Howard chose to emphasise the English-speaking aspect of his integration plan, announcing changes to Australia's migration policies that made it harder for non-English speakers to become Australian citizens. The changes would not be a problem for 'fair dinkum' wannabe Aussies, and the changed English language test was a natural extension of Australian 'values'.[15]

'I can't understand how anybody can take exception to that,' he said at the time. 'I mean the great unifying thing about this country is language, I mean our culture, the culture of any country is heavily defined by its language. Because along with the language comes the literature and the cultural history bound up with it.'[16]

It had the desired effect. In 2008, under the Labor government, figures were released showing people from Sudan, Afghanistan and Iraq struggled the most with the Howard test, with failure rates of 29.6 per cent, 24.9 per cent and 16 per cent respectively, whereas 97 per cent of 'skilled' migrants passed first go.[17]

'It won't become more difficult if you're fair dinkum and most people who come to this country are fair dinkum about becoming part of the community,' Howard said at the time. 'I think most people will welcome it – you'll certainly need to know a good deal more about Australia and about Australian customs and the Australian way of life.'[18]

We've seen that time and time again. Peter Dutton, a student of Howard's, said he believed Malcolm Fraser had 'made a mistake' in allowing Lebanese people to settle in Australia.[19] Liberal senator Jane Hume openly implied Chinese–Australians assisting with political campaigns were spies. The Indian–Australian community became the target of 'March for Australia' anti-immigration rallies in 2025, and Liberal senator Jacinta Nampijinpa Price refused to apologise for falsely claiming Indian migration was being bolstered to prop up Labor's vote.

Losing the prime ministership has done nothing to change Howard's mind. In 2021, in response to a survey carried out by the national broadcaster, which found 76 per cent of Australians believed there was underlying racism in Australia, Howard fervently disagreed and said that 'has not been my experience'. Shocking as it may be that an upper-middle-class white man hasn't experienced racism, Howard, who was voted Australia's 'best prime minister' in the same poll, has at least remained consistent.

And one consequence has been that it was under Howard that calling someone a racist became a worse crime than actually being racist. Howard has spent his life taking offence at anyone who has ever labelled him a racist. In 1998, he told journalist Ray Martin that 'those sort of comments have hurt me a lot', followed by:

> Well, I suppose I can just hope that people understand that my, the character of my life and the association that I've built with people of all different races and backgrounds and the tolerance that I practise. I mean, what really matters is how you live your life not a particular label that's put on you, but those sort of labels can be hurtful and I have found that one, and still do, deeply offensive because I don't have a racist bone in my body and I do find that extraordinarily offensive and it is against everything that I've always sort of believed about the equality of men.[20]

Which is true, as long as the 'equality of men' is what Howard considers to be equality.

In 2023, while urging Australians to vote 'no' in the Voice referendum and expressing his troubles with multiculturalism, Howard again said he just didn't see the point: 'I think one of the problems with multiculturalism is we try too hard to institutionalise differences, rather than celebrate what we have in [common].' The fact that institutions might be needed to counterbalance racism or discrimination completely escapes him. Why would you need institutions to protect minorities in a country where everyone naturally has the same values?

Howard gave Australians permission to be racist – as long as it wasn't too overt. Pointing out racism is something those politically correct elites did, and they just didn't understand the good ole Australian values that were instinctual to fair dinkum Aussies like Howard and his voters. It doesn't matter how much data shows racism not only exists in Australia, it flourishes – impacting everything from our public debate to our institutions and who is allowed to direct them, and the impacts to our very identity – John Howard didn't experience racism and therefore it can't be real. To say that is racist, or *gasp* is white privilege in action, is not only *hurtful*, it reveals what is *actually* wrong with this country. Hasn't Harmony Day taught us anything?

4
Indigenous Rights

> 'The debate over Australian history [. . .] risks being distorted if its focus is confined only to the shortcomings of previous generations. It risks being further distorted if highly selective views of Australian history are used as the basis for endless and agonised navel-gazing about who we are or, as seems to have happened over recent years, as part of a "perpetual seminar" for elite opinion about our national identity. The current debate over Australian history would benefit from a more balanced approach, from a wider perspective and from less pre-ordained pessimism. In the broad balance sheet of our history, there is a story of great Australian achievement to be told.'[1]
>
> John Howard, 1996

It is not a stretch to say that the group who suffered the most under John Howard, and who continue to live the impacts of his legacy, are Indigenous Australians.

Not only do First Nations Australians have to live with all the structural changes the rest of us have inherited, their history and very existence formed the basis of one of Howard's first culture wars.

It is impossible to underestimate the harm Howard inflicted, not just on Indigenous people themselves, but on how the nation thinks of its Indigenous history.

In the decades leading up to Howard's election, the nation had been inching towards reckoning with its treatment of Indigenous Australians; a pathway to reconciliation and Indigenous self-determination was in sight.

The then prime minister, Paul Keating, had made it clear that white Australia needed to accept responsibility for its colonial beginnings and what followed. The High Court had rejected the concept of terra nullius at the time of British colonisation and upheld that Indigenous rights to the land had not been wholly lost upon colonisation – meaning that native title had not been extinguished by the British invasion.

Howard showed up to the Reconciliation Convention determined to let Indigenous Australians know a new leader was in town, and that he held a very different view to his predecessor.

Much like the Uluru Statement from the Heart, the event was years in the making. It was meant to map out the pathway to reconciliation, but Howard made it immediately clear he did not believe there was anything white Australia needed to reconcile:

> In facing the realities of the past, we must not join those who would portray Australia's history since 1788 as little more than a disgraceful record of imperialism [. . .] such an approach will be repudiated by the overwhelming majority of Australians who are proud of what this country has achieved although inevitably acknowledging the blemishes in its past history.[2]

Describing the murder, displacement, forcible removal, enslavement and ongoing discrimination of Indigenous people as a 'blemish' was too much for many Indigenous delegates, who turned their backs on the new prime minister.

For Howard, it could not have gone better. He used the righteous response to start blowing his trumpet at relaxed and comfortable Australia – they didn't have to worry about feeling guilty or examining their prejudices while he was around.

Howard started as he meant to go on. Three years later he would refuse to participate in the Walk of Reconciliation, while still claiming he was working to 'heal the rift' between White and Indigenous Australia. He was the reason the rift had deepened, and certainly the reason reconciliation was derailed. He used the push back against his actions and words as proof he was trying to find common ground, he was simply rejected by those who refused to see sense.

In that, he also set up the perfect foundation.

The Mabo ruling in 1992 sent a wave of unease across a white Australia that was used to not having to consider the impact of its origins on the original inhabitants. By the time of the Wik ruling in 1996, which expanded on the Mabo decision and found the pastoral licences did not necessarily extinguish native title (recognising co-existing rights), Howard was in control of the nation. Despite the High Court ruling that in the case of conflict between pastoral leases and native title, the pastoral lease would prevail (although still not extinguish native title), Howard used the ruling as a match to reignite racial tensions against Indigenous people. Indigenous rights appeared to be the easiest way Howard could launch his war on 'political correctness', which other than industrial relations and changing the tax system, was his main driver for power.

He went on ABC's *7.30 Report* where he claimed that 78 per cent of Australia was 'at risk' from native title claims (the ruling had nothing to do with freehold land). 'The Labor Party and the Democrats are effectively saying that the Aboriginal people of Australia should have the potential right of veto over further development of 78 per cent of the land mass of Australia,' he said, holding up a marked-up map.[3]

No one was saying that, but it set the tone and changed the debate almost overnight. Talkback radio became inflamed by people claiming suburban backyards were next (something Howard refused to rule out by saying he didn't know if it were possible as there had been no legal test case yet).[4] The mining industry jumped on board. The National Farmers' Federation president at the time, Donald McGauchie, said 'the decision has just about ended Aboriginal reconciliation'.[5]

There was no truth to any of it, but it didn't matter. Howard had found the match to spark his culture war, and he used it to start dividing 'us' and 'them' in earnest.

He had already slashed $470 million in funding from the Aboriginal and Torres Strait Islander Commission (ATSIC) and appointed an administrator who took control over the board and its functions. That funding cut led to a 30 per cent reduction in programs, but Howard was able to take advantage of perceptions that ATSIC was simultaneously failing to deliver while also giving too much, to start pulling back.[6] That done (the first domino in the body being scrapped entirely), Howard started in on native title and self-determination, as well as dismissing any suggestion of an apology.

Howard obviously understood the power of feeling connected to the past and the environment. He drenched Australia in jingoism, insisting his version of what mattered in Australia's history become what mattered to everyone: Captain Cook, Weary Dunlop, Don Bradman. In 1988, moving into what was then called 'New Parliament House' as opposition leader, Howard insisted the furniture in the opposition leaders' suite be replaced because it was 'too progressive' for a conservative party. The suite had not been designed with party politics in mind. The architect who designed the suite, John Smith Murdoch, wrote in a scathing submission to a parliamentary inquiry about the changes that:

> The suite was not designed for him, or the Liberal Party, or any other party. It was designed for the Office of Leader of the Opposition, which would change its political hue across several parties no doubt during its lifetime. The suite was designed to reflect the role of opposition, which is essentially a relatively radical role in that it is charged with testing the sitting government and destabilising its possible complacency.[7]

Howard did not care. When he became prime minister, he and wife Janette again upended tradition for their own comfort, removing the specially designed furniture from the prime minister's suite and insisting Robert Menzies's desk be hauled from Old Parliament House and installed in Howard's official office. In a perfect metaphor for how Howard ruled, they didn't care enough about preserving history to ensure it remained untouched. Menzies's desk was for a much taller man and therefore had to be cut down to fit Howard's shorter frame.[8] But for the Howards, it was the principle. Menzies was a giant of a man, who believed in true liberalism ideals. He listened to Nugget Coombs, delivered full employment (albeit for white men) and kept in place Labor policies he believed would deliver for the country. In contrast, Howard was short in stature and compromise but promoted himself as the heir of the Menzies legacy – everyone who loved Menzies could be relaxed and comfortable in thinking his legacy was in safe hands. The image of Howard hacking away at Menzies's desk so he could fit under it sums up his prime ministership in one symbolic move.

Howard didn't stop at the desk though. Janette Howard forced public servants to replace the suite's specially designed furniture with whatever her husband preferred, which, from photos, appeared to be leather chesterfields most often seen in turn-of-the-century gentlemen's clubs. (You could imagine the public outcry if a Labor politician pulled this sort of stunt and how it would have been seen as shitting all over Australia's history and placing their own desires over that of the parliament, a building owned for, and by, the people.)

It's important to know this because it provides some context. Howard did understand a connection to the past. He did understand the importance of history. It was crucial to him that his environment reflected that importance and that anyone who entered his space was not only immediately made aware of the significance of that history, but that they also understood who Howard was. It was very important that Howard had control over his spaces – so important, he changed the country to better reflect his version of history.

He just didn't care for anyone else's history. Especially if that history contradicted the narrative he was setting up or required taking responsibility. It was why Geoffrey Blainey's 'black armband' and the false narrative of needing to 'correct' a pendulum that had swung too far in one direction was so attractive to Howard. That was a story he could easily sell, and he did. But it was Indigenous Australians who paid the price, just as they had since settlement.

With public anger swirling over the Wik decision, egged on by false and deliberately misleading narratives from vested interests, Howard came up with his 'Ten Point Plan' to legislate Wik out of relevancy. Wik itself didn't actually change anything – and for Indigenous people, it was a conservative ruling that upheld the status quo. It only made clear, in the black letter of the law, that pastoral rights did not extinguish native title, although native title rights counted for very little, if anything, in the event of competing rights over the land.

But despite its lack of real-world impact, Howard vowed to neuter any and all implication that native title could matter. But, holding on to the lessons of 1988 where he was going too hard and saying all the quiet parts out loud, Howard blew his dog whistle lightly. Following his negotiations with the Nationals on the wording of his plan (it shouldn't surprise you that Indigenous communities were not consulted), Howard said:

> Indigenous leaders have repeatedly been told by me that pastoralists and farmers must be guaranteed the right to carry on their normal day to day activities without fear of interference or hindrance.
>
> My aim has always been to strike a fair balance between respect for native title and security for pastoralists, farmers and miners. That is one reason why I staunchly oppose blanket extinguishment of native title on pastoral leaseholds.
>
> The fact is that the Wik decision pushed the pendulum too far in the Aboriginal direction. The Ten Point Plan will return the pendulum to the centre.[9]

There is that pendulum again. Wik didn't move it at all, but that inconvenient truth would have allowed Howard to move it even further back.

The leader of the Nationals and Howard's deputy, Tim Fischer, didn't need to beat around the bush with his constituency and openly admitted the Plan was meant to deliver 'bucket loads of extinguishment'. The plan led to two years of debate, mostly because Howard refused to compromise on elements of the plan until 1998, when it became obvious that One Nation was on the march in Queensland and using the lack of movement on the Wik legislation to stir up political divides within the conservatives. A deal was done with independent senator Brian Harradine and Howard had his bill.

Two decades later and Indian multinational conglomerate Adani was using native title 'issues' to lobby the Turnbull government for faster approvals for its Queensland coal mines.[10] Turnbull, with bipartisan support from Labor, further amended native title legislation to address those 'concerns'.[11] This also happened without consultation from Indigenous communities.

While Howard waged war on the Wik decision, he also had to deal with the inquiry into the Stolen Generations, which his government had inherited from Paul Keating's.

Despite his own love of the past that had shaped him, Howard was incapable of seeing how government policy could shape future outcomes when it came to taking responsibility for generational inequality. Howard spent his life shamelessly denying the need to feel shame; and nowhere was this clearer than in his response to *Bringing them Home*, the National Inquiry into the Separation of Aboriginal and Torres Strait Islander Children from their Families.

The moment the report and its recommendations were handed down, Howard set the tone, making it clear there would be no apology for the Australian government's past actions in stealing Indigenous children from their families and working to ensure they lost language, culture and connection to their loved ones and Country, while also continuing to treat them as second-class citizens in the world they had been forced into.

'I speak for the entire government on this, and it's a matter that's been discussed at great length,' he said on ABC's *7.30 Report* in 2000. 'We don't think it's appropriate for the current generation of Australians to apologise for the injustices committed by past generations.'[12]

Howard still refuses to acknowledge his lack of empathy for Indigenous people. In 2008, during one of his first speaking tours in the United States, Howard said he felt no regrets for not apologising because the policy had been created with what he thought were good intentions. His successor, Kevin Rudd, had made apologising one of his first acts after winning the election. Howard would refer to that as a 'box ticking' exercise. One of Howard's protégés, Peter Dutton, boycotted the apology, something he was later forced to apologise for when his own leadership ambitions necessitated apologising for previous versions of himself.

Speaking with students at Harvard University a month after Rudd's apology, Howard stated: 'I do not believe, as a matter of principle, that one generation can accept responsibility for the acts of an earlier generation. I don't accept that as a matter of principle.'[13] This is despite wanting to enshrine total respect for his chosen heroes across the nation.

He continued, saying, 'In some cases, children were wrongly removed; in other cases, they were removed for good reason; in other cases, they were given up; and in other cases, the judgment on the removal is obscure or difficult to make.'

Howard's belief that the report only told one side of the story (the only side of the story that mattered, but that never came into it) is not surprising given it was the line his government used to keep people relaxed and comfortable about their nation's past actions.

His Aboriginal and Torres Strait Islander Affairs minister, John Herron, had called the report 'one-sided', and dismissed it as focusing 'only on one view of the separation process'.

The same man who wanted every Australian to know the name of Don Bradman, to hold James Cook on a pedestal, who wanted Robert Menzies (Howard's version) worshipped, and who created culture wars over any criticism of the way he saw the world, found it too difficult to make a judgement over whether government policy had a negative impact on a group of people still disadvantaged as a result of that policy and others like it.

Howard was also concerned that saying the word 'sorry' would open the government up to compensation claims and so made sure the word did not leave his lips when he delivered a statement of 'regret' to the parliament to try and end the firestorm of controversy his reaction to the report had started.

Pauline Hanson was well entrenched in these issues by now and spent her time talking about the nonsensical 'reverse racism' that Indigenous people were apparently benefiting from – something she had used in the days after her election and was able to deploy with even more effect in the first three years of Howard's leadership. That was helped along by Howard and his government refusing to accept not just the need for an apology, but also one of the core findings of the report – that genocide had been exercised against Indigenous Australians as a result of the policy Howard couldn't say had been harmful.

Howard said he didn't believe a genocide had taken place and he still didn't. It's not clear what he considered the end goal of forcibly removing children from their families and homes, banning them from speaking their languages or practising their customs and forcing them to assimilate was, if not to end Indigenous culture, but Howard has never truly had to explain why he holds the beliefs he does.

Frank Bongiorno, a noted Australian Professor of History, made the point in his review of the 1996/97 Cabinet documents release that it was One Nation voters that the Howard government was most concerned about 'bringing home', and there is little evidence to prove him wrong.

Not content with deliberately stirring up false fears over the Wik decision, slashing funding to the Indigenous advisory body ATSIC and then eventually scrapping it altogether, refusing to apologise to Indigenous people for the Stolen Generations or acknowledge the policy amounted to genocide, Howard then created the conditions for the federal government 'intervention' in Northern Territory Indigenous communities.

The *Little Children are Sacred* report, commissioned by the Northern Territory Government in 2006, combined with the sensationalist media reporting by the ABC's *Lateline* program, helped create the the political climate Howard would later seize on. After the June 2007 report was handed down, Howard sprang into action, claiming his government would intervene to 'protect Aboriginal children from sexual abuse and family violence'. His government did not consult with Aboriginal people as it gave itself the power to take Aboriginal land for at least five years and apply financial controls to welfare payments, heavily regulating the lives of people in seventy-three Indigenous communities.

Uniformed soldiers were sent in by the federal government, and the *Racial Discrimination Act 1975* was suspended as part of the 'emergency' intervention. Alcohol and pornography were banned. Welfare was linked to children's school attendance. Successful Indigenous programs were scrapped and their employees forced into unemployment, and therefore the welfare controls. Police presence was increased in the communities and Indigenous customs were no longer to be considered as part of court and bail hearings.

The Labor opposition, by then so cowed by almost eleven years of Howard's successful run of culture wars, did not see any electoral gain in pushing back against the so-called 'national emergency'. Indigenous leaders and experts were ignored. Labor ended up extending parts of the Howard policy, including the quarantined welfare payments, which the later Morrison government attempted to expand and was then rebranded under a different name by the Albanese Labor government.

It was the final nail in the coffin for any hope of Indigenous self-determination. The lack of evidence-based policy did not seem to bother anyone but the experts and Indigenous communities, and politicians continue to use Indigenous communities as scapegoats for government failures to address root causes.

The Voice to Parliament referendum campaign, which the Coalition (under Peter Dutton and David Littleproud) opposed purely for political reasons, saw the intervention revisited by the Liberal Party, who began pushing for momentum for a Royal Commission into the areas the *Little Children are Sacred* report had covered.

The Voice referendum failed in every jurisdiction other than the ACT. After the results, the Coalition dropped any pretence of looking for the 'actual' solutions for the disadvantages Indigenous people continue to experience. Howard, who had gone to his final election promising to start the process towards Indigenous recognition in the Constitution, campaigned against the Voice, falsely claiming it created 'racial divides' and the possibility of 'judicial adventurism' by adding them to the Constitution.

The same man who had wanted to include 'mateship' in the preamble to the Constitution was suddenly afraid that including Indigenous people in the document (something he had once claimed to want to do himself) could be a legal problem.

After the apology, the Rudd government established the National Congress of Australia's First Peoples to represent Indigenous Australians. The newly elected Abbott Coalition government cut all funding to the congress in 2014.

The Voice campaign run by the Coalition was one of the most recent examples of the Howard playbook in action. As the linear nature of time naturally slows Howard down, Abbott is picking up his mantle, particularly when it comes to raising 'Western civilisation' over Indigenous history, picking up the culture war barrow and shoving it into any progress of reconciliation while blocking any and all attempts of Indigenous self-determination.

And Australia? It keeps letting them.

5
Asylum Seekers and Migration

> 'We will decide who comes to this country and the circumstances in which they come [. . .]'[1]
>
> John Howard, 2001

After the dismantling of the White Australia Policy, there had largely been a consensus between the two major parties when it came to multiculturalism in Australia. That included asylum seekers.

Enter John Howard.

The year 1988 may have proven too early to be so overtly racist in Australia, but by the time the times suited Howard in the late 90s, Australia was much more inclined to hear him out.

The 'One Australia' policy within Howard's ill-fated 'Future Directions' document had spelt out that Howard expected migrants to 'accept our social mores and laws, respect the institutions and principles basic to Australian society [and] want to integrate into this society'.[2] In 1988 there was no doubt who Howard meant when he spoke of wanting migrants to 'integrate'; in later comments to the media he said he wanted migration from Asia to be 'slowed down a little, so the capacity of the community to absorb it was greater'.[3] Historian Geoffrey Blainey, who was also responsible for Howard's co-opting of the 'black armband' of history, had said much the same thing in 1984.[4]

So it should have come as no surprise that the moment Howard felt he had enough social licence to act on some of his long-held impulses, he did.

That was one of the things seemingly missed at the time of the Howard prime ministership – many commentators seemed surprised that the mild mannered, shockingly ordinary conservative who finally made it to the Lodge (or in his case, Kirribilli) after decades of hard slog and setbacks in politics, had seemingly morphed into such a hard man on so many issues.

But reading history, there were no surprises. Everything Howard did to change Australian society had been previewed in his earlier years in politics. He did everything he said he would do. It's just sometimes, he claimed to have changed his views on some of the more contentious issues when he needed to get elected. It may seem shocking that the man who has said he always had trouble with the concept of multiculturalism wanted to put limits on permanent migration and asylum seekers, but stay with us here.

Economic insecurity and global uncertainty saw an increase of asylum seekers attempting to reach Australia by boat. They were very quickly dubbed 'illegal' (it is not illegal to seek asylum) and were referred to as 'boat people'. Temporary protection visas had been previously established, with the intention of deterring people hoping to receive permanent residency in Australia by a Howard government that had inelegantly flopped over the line for its second election win. In 2000, fifty-one boats with 2939 passengers arrived in Australia, including twelve boats in the last two weeks of the year, carrying 800 people. By August 2001, it had become a manufactured 'crisis', with the people being housed in on-shore mandatory detention, grabbing headlines and sympathy from the Australian people, who had begun to swing against the government.

Then came the Norwegian freighter the MV *Tampa* carrying 433 asylum seekers that its captain and crew had rescued after responding to the emergency mayday calls from the *Palapa*, a stranded Indonesian fishing boat in the Indian Ocean.

Captain Arne Rinnan rescued the mostly Hazara asylum seekers from Afghanistan and set course for the closest dock, which in this case was the Indonesian city of Merak. But the distress of his new passengers, many of whom threatened suicide if forced to return to Indonesia, convinced the captain to set course for Australian waters.

Howard decided to use the *Tampa* to 'draw a line on what is increasingly becoming an uncontrollable number of illegal arrivals in this country' and refused to accept the ship.[5] Many of the asylum seekers were ill, but for forty-eight hours, Rinnan's repeated requests for assistance from Australia were ignored. Worried about the health of his new passengers, and his crew, he made the decision to enter Australian territory, even without the permission of the government, and was told he was in 'flagrant breach' of the law. Special Air Service (SAS) troops were sent by the government to intercept and board the boat and prevent it from reaching Christmas Island. While cranky Australian SAS troops were reluctantly seeing to the asylum seekers at Rinnan's insistence, the Howard government was hastily trying to change the law to give his government the power to remove ships from Australian waters. *The Border Protection Bill 2001* had been backdated to include the *Tampa* and attempted to give full immunity for any Australian military officer in removing any foreign ships. The Senate said no, and Howard turned to plan B. After three days trying to shove its border bill through the parliament, it made agreements with the Pacific Island nations of Nauru and New Zealand to accept the asylum seekers. New Zealand took 131. The other 302 people were sent to Nauru, where some remained for three years. The whole thing, from when Rinnan first sighted the stranded ship, to when the government made the deal for Nauru and New Zealand to accept Australia's responsibility, had taken a little over a week.

Rinnan was lauded as a hero when he returned to Norway for how he had handled the situation and for upholding international law in the face of unprecedented pressure from the Australian government. The international community was shocked.

And then came September 11, 2001, and the world mostly forgot.

Howard used the sudden shift in public attitudes to Muslims and Arabs to set up what we know as the 'Pacific Solution', which cut off Christmas Island and other offshore Australian territories from Australia's migration zone. This meant any asylum seeker who made it to one of the islands would not have the right to apply for refugee status. Asylum seekers who arrived by boat would no longer be processed for asylum in Australia and were sent to Nauru or Manus Island. Mandatory detention became mandatory *offshore* detention.

Labor, at this point completely cowed on the issue following September 11, did not push back. It was barely mentioned in Labor leader Kim Beazley's election campaign launch, while Howard made tough on borders and national security his party's whole identity. Labor voters saw nothing to believe in, while Howard expanded his 'middle', picking up some more of One Nation's voters. Hanson had said, 'I should have the right to have a say in who comes into my country', in her 1996 first speech to parliament.[6] The vibe, if not the words themselves, must have stuck with Howard, and he made 'we will decide who comes to this country and the circumstances in which they come' his 2001 election slogan.[7]

Then in October of that year, Howard, along with his staunch lieutenants Philip Ruddock and Peter Reith, lied and said asylum seekers attempting to reach Australia had deliberately thrown their children overboard, into the ocean, to try and force rescue and passage to Australia.

The story went that the HMAS *Adelaide* had stopped a wooden boat (which was called Suspected Irregular Entry Vessel 4 or SIEV 4 in the official reports) and soon after the boat sank. Ruddock spoke to the media the next day (which was the day before the 2001 election was called) and claimed he had information that the passengers on the boat threatened to throw their children into the ocean if they were forced to turn back. Howard and the then defence minister, Reith, also made the claim, using photos of children in the water as their proof. It became known as 'children overboard' and the Howard government, campaigning as 'strong' on border protection (in contrast to their 'weak' opponents) were returned to power with an increased majority.

A Senate inquiry into the affair, held after the election, found there was no evidence of any threats to throw children in the water or that any children were thrown, and that the government had known all of this before the election. Howard trebled down and said he would not apologise for his false accusations because 'they irresponsibly sank the damn boat, which put their children in the water'.[8] This also wasn't true, with the accepted position that the strain of being towed by HMAS *Adelaide* put too much pressure on the boat, and it sank. The photos the government had used as its evidence to show that children had been thrown into the water had been taken *after* the boat sank.

Given the public outcry at what they felt was their government deliberately misleading them over the affair, Howard claimed in *The Howard Factor* (published after his 2004 election win), 'if I had have been told definitively, if I had been told that that story was completely wrong, I would have said so, but I wasn't.'[9] In the same interview, he added – just in case he wasn't overt enough by claiming that these were the sort of people who would deliberately put their children in danger by sinking a boat (which they didn't do) – that the Iraqi refugees '[didn't] carry any visible signs of being demonised'.[10]

A former advisor to Reith revealed in 2004 that he had told Howard about his doubts over the 'children overboard' claim. Howard called for an election less than two weeks later. He romped it in there too, as well as winning the Senate for the first time.

Howard had changed the way Australia saw asylum seekers, making what is still one of the world's cruellest mandatory detention policies seem normal. So normal in fact that people will still argue it saved lives and 'stopped the boats', and all but forced a paralysed Labor into accepting it as a bipartisan position. In 2025, the Albanese government announced its third country solution to deporting people whose visas had been cancelled, or denied, but who couldn't be sent to their country of origin. The announcement, which will see more than a billion dollars paid to Nauru to reopen an offshore detention facility, barely made a ripple.

At the same time as Howard was demonising asylum seekers and refugees, channelling public disgruntledness and hate towards one of the globe's most vulnerable cohort, he turbocharged migration.

Migration numbers in 2007 were almost double what they were in 1996 (as a proportion of population), which neatly coincided with Australia's mining boom.[11] Now, it's a political truism (that's actually true) that Liberal governments will always support higher migration (neolibs just love wage suppression through importing cheaper labour, while also ensuring more consumers for traditional allies in big business), but that doesn't mean that they make life easy for them.

Howard had no problem with migration as long as it was temporary and served the interests of business. So while stoking public suspicion of 'them', ramping up the jingoism and making 'tough on borders' Australia's national anthem, Howard switched up the nation's migration program from one which addressed humanitarian or community concerns (like family reunion visas) to one which focused on business.

Family reunion visa entries shrank from 80 per cent in 1998 to roughly 20 per cent by 2013. But don't worry! The 'Contributory Parent visa' meant those who could afford to pay more could get ahead of the artificially long queue and bring mum and dad out to Australia.

Humanitarian visas dropped to numbers lower than what they had been under Keating.[12]

The citizenship test was introduced for anyone who had made it to the point of being able to apply for naturalisation. Previously, it had been an interview. The test was designed to be easy for a certain kind of migrant – one who spoke English almost like a native speaker, who understood what mostly white, natural-born Australians knew about their culture and life, and who had whatever skills the government had decided to import. We had gone from the country of the fair go to a fair go for some, and only under our terms.

We're still having 'debates' about migration and we are still blaming migrants for the failures in government policy to keep up with infrastructure, services and housing needs. We still blame asylum seekers for needing asylum and not doing it the 'right way', because governments since Howard have convinced us the 'right' way is easy. We still don't consider the desperation involved in paying someone every cent we have for passage on a leaky boat heading towards an uncertain future, or how hopeless life must seem that risking your children on that same leaky boat, is the better option.

The Coalition has continued its hard right turn on immigration and asylum policy. Tony Abbott oversaw 'Operation Sovereign Borders'. Scott Morrison had a statue of a boat with 'I stopped these' in his office. A decade and a half on from 'children overboard', Morrison falsely claimed that staff from independent aid agency Save the Children had coached asylum seekers being held offshore on how to self-harm and used children in protests. He also came up with 'on-water matters' to stop anyone from finding out just what Australia's defence ships were doing in the name of so-called 'border protection'.

Peter Dutton accused asylum seekers detained offshore of making up false rape claims in order to come to Australia for medical treatment. In 2022, in a last-ditch attempt to turn voters his way, Morrison delivered his own last-minute pre-election boat scare. (It didn't work.) In what would be one of Scott 'I stopped the boats' Morrison's last acts as prime minister, he instructed Border Force to announce its interception of a suspected asylum seeker boat on election day, to enforce his point that people smugglers were celebrating a Labor government. In 2022, voters saw through the blatantly politically act in a way they had not in 2001. Howard's policy, though, went international.

Abbott went on a speaking tour in the UK promoting his 'stop the boats' campaign and both the Tories and Labour adopted similar third-country resettlement approaches. Donald Trump said in 2019 he thought 'much can be learned' from Australia's hardline border policies, and in 2025 was deporting undocumented Americans to El Salvador.

Howard's greatest legacy in this space is that he spooked Labor into following suit. After Kevin Rudd vowed to end offshore detention in 2007, Labor reintroduced offshore processing in 2012, goaded by Abbott's non-stop attacks that it was 'weak' on borders. It remains policy. Voters also believe in the Coalition's spin on Australia's migration numbers, and its claim that Labor had allowed migration to 'get out of control'. Despite the numbers showing migration has normalised to just under the predicted 2025 figure, the Coalition has falsely blamed migration, including international students, for the housing crisis and general congestion. Labor has done very little to push back, even as Nazis spoke at anti-migration rallies held across the country.

The main crackdown has been on those who attempted to counter the anti-immigration March for Australia message.

Howard reopened Australia's cruel streak and turned it into an open wound. There's been very little attempt to heal it in the time since he's left office.

6

Privatisation

'[Medicare has] raped the poor in this country.'[1]

John Howard, 1987

To understand Australia's twenty-fifth prime minister's attitude towards public services, look no further than Medicare.

The man was not a fan of universal health care. Not because he was against people having health care in general, but because he didn't think everyone should pay for everyone else to have access to it. Howard liked to call himself an 'economic liberal' and a 'social conservative', as if the two naturally complemented each other. But in reality, he was neither. Howard's politics have always been different shades of conservatism dressed up in terms to make it seem like he wasn't so one-eyed.

But much like his war on political correctness or identity politics (which only ever went one way: anyone who agreed with his side of the ledger was obviously just sensible, while anyone pushing against it was too radical and PC for words), his economics was centred around his own worldview.

If you wanted health insurance, then you should pay for it – and it was not the job of the state to look after that for you. And if you couldn't afford it, well too bad – you should work harder to prove you're deserving of the nation's largesse.

That was pretty much his (and that of many other Liberals at the time) opinion on universal health care in a nutshell. After a few false starts, Gough Whitlam's government pushed through the Medibank legislation, which became the fledgling beginnings of Medicare. Malcolm Fraser's government then abolished it. Bob Hawke's brought it back. As opposition leader, Howard vowed to 'stab it' in the guts. He declared that he didn't need to stab Medicare in the back, as the government claimed, because he was open about killing it.

In a doorstop interview ahead of the 1987 election campaign, Howard responded to then-treasurer Paul Keating's statements that Howard's proposed cuts in health care would cost Australians $27 a week with the hyperbole that would serve him well in later years:

> Absolute nonsense. Everybody knows that one of the great disasters of the Hawke government has been Medicare. It's raped the poor in this country. There are a hundred thousand Australians on the waiting

> queues of the public hospital system. Everybody resents having to pay twice under Medicare, which you do. This country needs a better, more efficient, more competitive and a fairer health delivery system and they'll get it from us when we win the election.[2]

He did not win the election. By the time he did, just under a decade later, he had accepted that Medicare was popular with Australians and claimed his views had changed and he now supported the system.

Because if there was one thing Howard had, other than rat cunning and a nose for politics, it was knowing how to get what you wanted by coming from the side.

Medicare was sacrosanct. Every politician knew that, so Howard set about his privatisation process by another method – undermining the public system, by artificially propping up the private one.

In what seemed like a very benign question of *¿Por qué no los dos?* when it came to public and private, Howard introduced the first of his carrots and sticks to push people into buying private health insurance.

Thirty years ago, private health insurance was only for the wealthy, or for those who needed the extras (like dental) not covered under the universal offering. Howard changed that by introducing the Commonwealth's 30 per cent rebate for private health insurance in 1999 (replacing the short-lived 1997 private health insurance incentive scheme, which did not incentivise enough according to Howard), which meant that the Commonwealth reimbursed 30 cents of every dollar spent on private health insurance by anyone eligible for Medicare (means testing began in 2012, but the scheme remains).

So suddenly private health insurance, which at the time had very few exclusions to what it covered, seemed a bargain for the middle class. And then came the stick.

In 2000, the Howard government introduced its Lifetime Health Cover policy, which meant that if you didn't purchase, and maintain, private health cover by the time you turned thirty-one, you would be forced to pay higher premiums if you made the decision to take it out in later life (2 per cent loading for every year you are aged over thirty-one, capped at 70 per cent).

And if that STILL didn't get you turning towards the private health system, there was the Medicare Levy Surcharge that forced people on higher incomes to pay for a certain level of private health insurance, or face a higher level of tax.

So much for small government, huh? Or economic liberalism, where people can make their own choices.

The result of Howard's intervention is what we see today. The government spends about $8 billion a year on the private health rebate, and exempting the private health insurance rebate from income tax costs another $1.6 billion.[3] So that's almost $10 billion a year that could be spent on public health, which isn't – because it's subsidising people who were forced into the private system. It's privatisation by stealth. And still, even with all that money spent, less than half of Australians have private health insurance.[4] Mostly because it's not worth the money they would lose in premiums.

For those who do have it, they realised that to get within the lifetime health cover frame, it was most beneficial to take out the minimum possible cover. That has created a surge in insurances with excesses and co-payments, from 30 per cent to 88 per cent (as of 2025).

Back in 1999, 95 per cent of people had private health cover with no exclusions. In 2025, about 65 per cent of private health policies available have exclusions, which means different treatments and items are not covered. Howard, who was upset in 1987 about 'poor' people being 'raped' by Medicare and having to pay twice – once in their tax and once in the gap – has created a system where people pay for Medicare, a gap, private health insurance and then that gap. Claps all round really. And at the same time, premiums have risen about 60 per cent above wages.

The system is now so unwieldy, all these issues are baked in.

This also explains how Howard helped privatise Australia's public education system. In much the same way he undermined public health, Howard undermined the public education system with the so-called 'economic liberal' prioritising private funding over public.

He abolished the Hawke-era 'new schools' policy, which withheld public funds from those who wanted to establish a non-government school in an area where there were already adequate schools, because no one should stop the private sector from setting up where they wished, even if it meant the public system suffered.

He then oversaw a new funding scheme, which replaced the Educational Resources Index (the ERI model) with a new socioeconomic status (SES) model. The ERI wasn't perfect, but it was at least based on the total private income of a school. The SES model determined the socioeconomic status of a school based on the address and how the ABS categorised the area the school serviced. It didn't take into account the private income of students' families, so rich kids from areas classified as having poorer socioeconomic status would get more money for the school. Additional funding was also guaranteed to any non-government school that might have been disadvantaged by the switch in funding models. It all meant more Commonwealth money could be funnelled into already wealthy private schools.

And funnel money it did. Federal funding to private schools increased by $1584 per student between 1999 and 2005, compared to just $261 per student in the public system over the same period.[5]

And if that wasn't enough, state governments went through a stage of closing or consolidating government schools over the same period, which resulted in more students being enrolled in non-government schools due to reduced public school availability.

As a result, enrolment in government schools has steadily declined. In 1996, 66 per cent of high school students went to a public school, in 2023, that number was 58 per cent (or about 150,000 fewer). It hasn't been as dramatic in primary schools, but there has still been a drop, from 74 per cent in 1996 to 69 per cent in 2023.[6]

Given student numbers and demands can help set the educational budget, it means that students in public schools are doubly disadvantaged when it comes to funding – once because money that could be spent on public education is being spent on non-government schools that don't need it (and are spending it on things like Olympic-sized swimming pools) and again while lower demand for public schools shaves the money spent on the sector even further.

Five private schools in New South Wales and Victoria spent more on new facilities in 2021 than half the nation's public schools, yet governments don't seem to think this is a problem.[7] Howard didn't scrap public education, but he made the alternative as attractive as possible by rerouting taxpayer funds.

Which is also how he helped change the university and training sector.

Unable to throw as much control around universities as he did the health care and public school system, which was almost entirely reliant on government funding,

Howard changed who got to run universities as the first step in undermining them.

Then–education minister Brendan Nelson forced state governments (which create universities through acts of their parliaments) to pass laws to change who sits on university councils. They did that by threatening to withhold Commonwealth funding for the institutions. After having won that battle, they then reduced the number of council members who were required to be democratically elected by staff, academic and student bodies. Universities were forced to replace those council members with members who had 'business and commercial' expertise, which, in Howard's language, meant the big consulting firms, the big banks and other giant business interests. Howard convinced the public that universities needed to be run like corporations, otherwise taxpayers were not receiving return on investment (because education and the flow-on benefits from that were apparently not enough).

So now we have Australia's major universities being run by big business and their networks, with little input from staff, students or academics. The result? Poorer student outcomes, with much more spent on consulting and marketing.[8] But that's not all, folks! Because you can't control the future unless you control the future of voters, so Howard set about making university a hell of a lot more expensive. He gave universities (which were now being run as a business) the power to lift their fee caps (setting a ceiling they mostly all immediately went to) and then introduced tiers that changed how much you paid, depending on what sort of degree you wanted.[9,10] Yay! Graduates started their careers with a lot more debt than they had previously, and if you were someone who had to work to support yourself through university, you more likely than not hit the income threshold for repayments while still studying, docking your pay even further. This hit even more students when Howard lowered the income threshold to just above the average full-time wage at the time, while simultaneously cutting welfare payments for students. Hey students! Take on more debt, start repaying it back earlier, and get less support while you learn, while your storied institution of learning is now run by a business and increasingly cowed by political and vested interests. What could go wrong?

As it turns out, quite a lot. As the Vice Chancellor of Western Sydney University, George Williams, wrote in 2024, the Albanese government inherited a mess: 'The system for setting university fees in the first place is broken and unfair. It needs urgent reform.'[11]

Between 2004 and 2024, the cost of doing a humanities degree at the University of Sydney increased by 333 per cent (although that was helped along by one of Howard's successors, Scott Morrison, and his Job-ready Graduates scheme, which has achieved nothing except increase the debt levels of humanities and arts students).[12]

It's not unusual to see university students lining up for a free meal. But even those services were significantly cut back by the Howard government, which, as part of its war on unions and universities, managed to get a two-for-one in abolishing the compulsory student union fee (it was about $250). The social services provided by student unions largely disappeared, with the idea they would be filled by the free market.

In 2005, the last year before Howard finally got his voluntary student unionism bill the numbers it needed to pass the Senate, university unions received $172.8 million in fees.[13] In just two years, it fell by $166 million.

It may shock you to learn that these services, which were either run for free or at prices students could afford, aren't exactly profitable, which is why they were being run by the student union and not the free market in the first place; and those free marketeers didn't rush in to fill the void. That includes things like childcare, which ANU attempted to fully privatise in 2024 – a move that would have made it unaffordable for parents to continue to study.[14]

Neutering the student union movement also helped cut down on the influence students had on university administration – the cherry on top for the Howard government. The result? Between 1996 and 2004, HECS fees increased by between 33 per cent and 122 per cent, students often require financial support from their families, and students have almost no advocates at their universities.[15] Something that continues to this day. The collective HECS debt held by the Commonwealth has increased thanks to the Howard policies, and the average HECS debt held by students has doubled this century.[16]

Having turned universities into as much of a business as he could, vocational education stood no chance, with Howard managing to create a market where private providers were incentivised to compete with publicly funded TAFEs, who were also made to compete with each other for 'clients' (previously known as 'students').

Howard changed how the TAFE sector was funded and set up 'growth funds' that gave money to registered training organisations, which also covered private providers who were able to offer the same certifications once quarantined for TAFE centres. We still continue to use this model.

At the same time, Howard introduced what was known as the 'user choice' policy, where apprentices were sent to the training institution of their employer's choice, not their own. Money began flowing through the private sector at the expense of public vocational training, which has led to some questionable training methods. In 2008, the Organisation for Economic Co-operation and Development (OECD) recommended Australia introduce a national assessment to ensure all vocational degree holders held the same standardised skills and competencies when they graduated, but this wasn't taken up.

Howard also combined apprenticeships with traineeships, which made it look like the number of apprentices being trained had jumped, when in actuality it included people doing Certificate IV in massage therapies. Traineeships grew, apprentices didn't. In 2006, no longer able to hide the domestic skills shortage, Howard changed the program again to Australian apprenticeships, which remains in place, but left future governments with the issue of how to train more domestic staff for industries like construction and manufacturing. That issue was compounded by Howard handing over what was taught in vocational training to the Industry Skills Council, which gave industry the influence to shape courses.

Of the 4000 registered training organisations in Australia, 3000 are private. Between 1997 and 2004, education funding was cut by 8 per cent, while in all other OECD nations funding was increased by 38 per cent (on average). Commonwealth funding per student hour for vocational education and training was cut by 24 per cent over the same period.[17]

So, if you ever wonder why it's so expensive to hire a tradie in Australia, you can thank Howard. His policies helped create a shortage; by making it harder for people to qualify and more expensive to study and train – and that's assuming the 'college' they attended was actually teaching certifiable skills and not just cashing in on student numbers.[18] And that was despite a mining boom, in which, for a brief moment in time, certain trades could rocket you to Australia's highest income earners.

Howard marketised vocational education, turned universities into businesses, undermined universal health care by funnelling money to the private sector, and gutted public school funding by doing much the same thing. That's what he did when he couldn't outright privatise a sector, because the social licence managed to hold him off just enough. But if you ever wondered why the care sector in Australia is mostly privatised, instead of being run by the government, you can once again thank JWH (although in the case of childcare, he received a very big assist from the Hawke government).

The McMahon government began funding childcare in 1972 for not-for-profit and local government providers, but in the 1980s and 1990s, attitudes shifted and the Hawke government extended government funding to the private for-profit sector. The idea was that the good old market would bring down prices. By the time the Howard government got its hands on the levers, the chance for publicly funded childcare was done.

By 2006, a privately listed Australian childcare provider, ABC Learning Centres, was receiving 44 per cent of its income from government subsidies (about $128 million worth). Its founder, Eddy Groves, was estimated to hold a private wealth of $260 million, and his business had become the largest publicly traded childcare provider in the world, with a market capitalisation of $2.6 billion. By 2008, it held 20–25 per cent of the Australian long day care market. Then in November 2008, it went into voluntary liquidation and the government had to spend millions in propping the centres up (on top of the $300 million it had already received in subsidies in 2008) until the end of the year, given the number of staff and parents who would have seen their lives upended by its failure. Fifty-five centres were closed at the end of 2008 and another 241 of the 400 or so ABC Learning had operating were considered unviable. The government spent another $34 million in keeping those centres open until March 2009, and then a further $70 million to cover entitlements for staff before a buyer could be found for the business. Labor had started the market-led process for childcare, and then the Howard government let it rip.[19] His government's introduction of the childcare benefit, which in essence gave parents a voucher they could use at any approved service, gave private providers an instant cash injection. ABC Learning had listed on the stock exchange shortly after the benefit was announced and soon began buying up small and independent providers. It had also opened its own training college in a nice little ecosystem of government subsidies and payments, which benefited the business more than any of their staff, students or clients. Anthony Albanese has said universal childcare is one of his government's priorities. Given how entrenched the private market is in the sector, it is almost impossible to see how it can be achieved. And as of 2025, millennials and gen Z are having to read articles about how to protect their children from child sex offenders who have infiltrated the childcare sector through the private sector.

Then we get to aged care. The federal government had been involved in funding aged care in some way or another since the 1950s, when Australia's hospital system switched from long care to mostly acute care. Funding for private providers began in the 1960s when a subsidy was introduced to lower the cost of places for residents.[20] By the time of the Labor government of the 1980s, new regulations were in place, which included a funding system that set out how much specifically was to be spent on care, separate to the other costs, but the majority of funding still went to not-for-profit providers. As state and local governments ceded the space to private providers, Labor made care subsidies available to for-profit providers, but maintained heavy regulations over how the money was to be spent.

The Liberal opposition sided with the for-profit providers who were lobbying to have the regulations lifted, with no success until 1997 and the Howard government's *Aged Care Act*. This ushered in the deregulation the private sector had been screaming for, and prioritised profit over patient care.

Howard stripped the sector of oversight and gave the private sector power over how it filled its staffing positions. Prior to Howard's changes, providers were made to prove they had spent a proportion of the funding they received from the government on care staff, which included skilled staff – such as registered nurses (RNs). There was also an attempt to install a user-pays system, which would have created tiers of care, but voter backlash forced the government to shelve the most controversial aspects.

Before 1997, the average aged care home was funded for and provided with just over 300 RN hours to residents.[21] By 2007, that number had fallen to 198. By the time of the royal commission into aged care, it was 168 hours a week.

Howard's slashing of 'red tape' had the desired effect – those wanting to make money flooded into the market. Private equity firms and investment banks have seen the sector as a safe bet for profit; Gabrielle Meagher, an Emeritus Professor at Macquarie University, reported in 2021 what Howard's changes meant:

> [. . .] in the years that followed, the for-profit share of residential care places increased from 27 per cent in 2000 to 41 per cent in 2019. Across these two decades, the number of places in residential care increased from around 140,000 to nearly 214,000, and more than two-thirds of this growth was in for-profit facilities. The share owned by non-profit providers (religious, charitable and community organisations) fell, from 63 to 55 per cent. Public provision collapsed, from

10 to 4 per cent, with nearly two out of every five public residential care places closed or sold.[22]

There were blaring alarm bells while Howard was still prime minister; a nursing home was closed after it was discovered that fifty-seven residents had been given diluted kerosene baths in 2000 as part of an archaic but cost-effective treatment for a scabies outbreak.[23] In 2019, it was revealed there were no regulations around restraints after an investigation found one man had been regularly strapped to a chair for fourteen hours a day.[24] Stories of elderly people being fed slop, or starved, left to sit in soiled clothes and bedding, bereft of human contact or care, unable to be showered or assisted to the bathroom, robbed, drugged, left in pain, given wrong medications – the list went on, until a royal commission ordered the return to mandated care hours, including with skilled staff such as RNs.

The process of reinstating skilled care began under the Albanese government in 2022, but the sector has been so demolished that the government had to stagger the implementation of the new policy to help find staff.

The government has had to step in and fund pay rises for both the aged care and early childhood education sectors in a bid to attract and maintain staff in two of the most notoriously underpaid sectors in Australia. This has all been the result of Howard's free market 'economic liberalism' that has seen people pay the cost.

That's how he treated the care economy, so are you surprised he also went out of his way to sell public assets like Telstra?

He claimed that was a 'promise kept' after vowing to do it in 1996. He managed it in 2006 thanks to young political up-and-comers like Barnaby Joyce who, then a Queensland Nationals senator, was against the sale, until he wasn't, helping to cinch Howard the numbers he needed.[25]

By the 2005/6 debate, the public had cooled on the idea of privatising the telco (thanks to lingering doubt over the privatisation of Qantas by the Labor government), but Howard pushed through as he had everything else, claiming it was an 'absurd conflict of interest' that the government was both the regulator and majority shareholder of Telstra:

> Governments are bad at running businesses . . . governments have no business running major corporations.
>
> Governments are there to govern in the public interest, they are not there to run companies, and it is in the long-term interest of the Australian people that this giant corporation be fully privatised.
>
> And I do not apologise for that. I do not take a back step on that.[26]

That argument didn't make sense then, or now. If he was so worried about a (manufactured) conflict of interest, he could have sold the retail part of the business but maintained the supply side. He didn't do that, because he wanted the money from the sale and it was all but worthless without the network.

The sale happened and Australia had no control over its telco, which put it in the ridiculous position of having to go cap in hand to Telstra in 2011, asking to buy its copper network for the national broadband network (despite taxpayers having paid for that network originally) and then paying Telstra to fix that copper network it sold for $11 billion, in 2015.[27]

So, you can add crap internet to the list of Howard sins as well.

7
Revenue and Managing the Economy

'Peter Costello and the Howard government got hit in the arse with a rainbow. He's just got to wake up every morning and take credit for the outcomes I created.'[1]

Former prime minister Paul Keating to Labor MP Mark Latham during a lunch at Keating's Sydney office, April 1999

Paul Keating wasn't wrong when he said Peter Costello, Howard's treasurer and deputy good boy, had been smacked in the derriere by luck when it came to the economy.

As much as Howard loves to take credit for his government creating the economic good times, it was, as so often has been the case historically for conservative governments in Australia, a matter of very good timing.

Even those who don't remember, or weren't here (or born) during the Howard years, have probably been told that Howard and Costello were 'excellent economic managers'. It's one of those truisms in Australian politics that it is just accepted, without any probing into whether it is true or not. The fact of the matter is, they weren't. Yes, Australia enjoyed excellent economic success during his eleven years of leadership, but very little of that can be attributed to Howard, and worst of all, he basically pissed it all up against a (tax cut) wall.

You don't have to go back too far to see that Howard's way of running the economy wasn't always sunshine and surpluses. He earned the derogatory nickname 'Honest John' during his time as treasurer under Malcolm Fraser. By the time his stewardship of the economy ended in 1983, inflation was running at 11 per cent (having peaked at 12.5 per cent), unemployment was sitting around 10 per cent, the Commonwealth fiscal deficit was 3.4 per cent of GDP and interest rates had reached 21.4 per cent in April 1982 – although it dropped back to around 11 per cent by the time he left the job a year later.[2]

No one remembers that though. They remember Paul Keating's 18 per cent interest rates and the fairly low interest rates under Howard–Costello. But go a little bit further back, and Honest John's handling of the economy (which, to be fair, was struggling under years of protectionist policies and a changing world order) wasn't exactly the gold standard. To quote Howard in 2004 as he was reminding people of interest rates under

Keating: 'I'm not making that up, it's not a scare tactic, it's a fact.'[3]

One that Costello knew – telling the authors of *John Winston Howard: The Biography*, Wayne Errington and Peter van Onselen: 'The Howard treasurership was not a success in terms of interest rates and inflation. He had not been a great reformer.'[4]

So why do we believe that Howard was a master economic manager? Mostly because people believe the story you tell them, and Howard and Costello told an *excellent* story about themselves. And also, because the mining boom and global economic times basically made it rain money.

Instead of investing that into services, or setting Australia up for the future, Howard and Costello embarked on tax cuts (mostly for the wealthy) and spending sprees that, without the increased revenue from the mining boom, would have put Australia straight back into a deficit. And we are still paying for it.

Imagine you won the lottery and then spent like you were going to keep winning the lottery and that's pretty much how Howard and Costello ran the federal Budget.

At the same time, they started convincing people that deficits were very bad, often making the analogy that 'just like the household budget', you had to 'spend within your means'. They were both fond of saying that you couldn't put everything on the credit card, and during the Howard years, the mark of a 'good' treasurer and a 'good' government became delivering a Budget surplus. This is a pretty big departure from the Menzies years, when he would argue while in opposition to John Curtin and Ben Chifley that he would have spent more and put the Budget further in the red in order to build even more houses than what Labor was doing at the time.

Howard slashed services and funding, baked in tax breaks for the wealthy and destroyed what was left of our progressive taxation system, with very little to show for it, despite the rainbow arse-slapping. He was so successful at convincing people he was a master economic manager that Labor's Kevin Rudd had to make being 'an economic conservative' part of his election brand.

Howard had nothing to do with Australian exports increasing from 4.5 per cent at the start of 1996 to 14 per cent at the end of 2007 – that was China's boom and Australia's luck at having the resources they needed.

It wasn't Howard who caused the price of Australian coal to rise 113 per cent from US$24.50/tonne at the end of 2002 to US$52.25/tonne at the end of 2004.[5]

Neither was Howard, or any of his policies, the reason why the world price of iron ore rose 414 per cent in the last three years of his government from US$37.90/tonne to US$195.09/tonne.

But while they couldn't claim credit for any of those once-in-a-generation circumstances, they did take credit for the increase in corporate tax revenue that began flowing into the Budget.

It also would have flowed into the Budget had Keating maintained power. But it happened under Howard and Costello, and here we are, living in an era of Howard myth-making.

Prior to 1999–2000 corporate tax revenue had never been greater than 4 per cent of GDP, and it had not been above 3.5 per cent of GDP since the 1950s and the commodity boom that occurred during and after the Korean War.

From 1999–2000 through the rest of the Howard government period, corporate tax revenue was never below 3.6 per cent of GDP, and in seven of the last eight years of his term of office it was above 4 per cent of GDP and in 2006–07 and 2007–08 it was above 5 per cent of GDP.

And it directly led to the delivery of Budget surpluses.

Chief economist at the Australia Institute, Greg Jericho, broke down what that meant: 'Consider that in 2001–02 when Howard and Costello delivered a budget deficit of 0.1 per cent of GDP, company tax revenue was 3.6 per cent of GDP. In 2006–07 when the budget surplus was 1.6 per cent of GDP, company tax revenue was 5.2 per cent of GDP or 1.6 per cent of GDP larger than it was in the deficit years.'[6]

So, do we have a super-fast train? Free higher education? An actual universal health system? Dental? A strong social safety net or affordable housing, or anything else you would expect from such luck at having incredible revenue flows?

Lol. That money was spent to deliver income tax cuts that left little time bombs in future Budgets and caused permanent damage to the budget position.

The Parliamentary Budget Office in 2013 reported that the structural budget balance had deteriorated over the last six years of the Howard government: 'Over two-thirds of the 5 percentage points of GDP decline in structural receipts over the period 2002–03 to 2011–12 was due to the cumulative effect of the successive personal income tax cuts granted between 2003–04 and 2008–09.'[7]

In public, Howard and Costello talked the big game about budget surpluses being the marker of good economic managers, but they spent their time delivering tax cuts that would send the Budget into deficit as soon as it no longer kept getting the huge booms in company tax.

They laid time bombs that would go off after they were no longer in charge, and for which they would not receive the blame. They both set up the parameters of 'good economic management' and then ensured no one else would be able to achieve it unless hit by another rainbow (as finally happened in 2022–23 with the surge in gas, coal and iron ore prices after the pandemic).

It was lazy economic management. And it's continued to fuck us. As Jericho said in an interview:

> One marker of how lazy the Howard surpluses were is that in the last eight Budget years which the Howard government delivered a surplus, total government revenue was never below 25 per cent of GDP – a level that was not reached once in the following thirteen years to 2021–22.
>
> The largest amount of revenue Wayne Swan had was 23.2 per cent of GDP in 2008–09 and in 2010–11 a mere 21.3 per cent of GDP was available to spend and company tax revenue had fallen from 5.2 per cent of GDP to 4 per cent – equivalent to a $17 billion drop in 2010–11 dollars.[8]

Budget surpluses should also be considered as money the government hasn't spent on people. A budget deficit is when they have maintained spending on people, even as revenue falls. Those numbers alone do not tell you anything about economic management – there is no context. Did money need to be spent, and it wasn't? Was money spent in the right places? Was it spent in the wrong places? Was it spent for the betterment of future generations? Was it preparing for the future? All of those questions matter.

But the Howard years have convinced a generation of Australians that the only thing that matters is surplus or deficit. Surplus = good, even as it drives the economy into the ground, and deficit = bad, even if it keeps the economy afloat. And the economy? It's people.

Some part of Howard and Costello acknowledge this. Let's look at 2001–02 when the dotcom bubble saw company tax revenue fall in one year from 4.5 per cent of GDP to 3.6 per cent. Rather than cut spending in an attempt to keep the Budget in surplus, they instead delivered a budget deficit that helped buoy the economy and prevented a fall into recession, as occurred in the United States.

Similarly, Josh Frydenberg's best year as treasurer was not when he nearly delivered a surplus and promised 'Back in Black', but when he did not cut spending during the lock down years but instead delivered the biggest deficits on record.

This, of course, was also the case for Wayne Swan; when he didn't slash spending in the face of the global financial crisis (GFC), but, with Rudd, undertook a large stimulus program that kept Australia out of a recession to such an extent that we still talk of the GFC, while those in America and Europe refer to the Great Recession.

Howard's time in office coincided with a good time for the global economy, which, combined with Australia's own mining boom, provided a double rainbow.

During his time in office, Australia's GDP rose on average 3.7 per cent a year – better than the 3.6 per cent average during Paul Keating's prime ministership and the 3.2 per cent that occurred during the Hawke years. Even more pointedly, during the Rudd–Gillard years that came straight after Howard, Australia's GDP rose just 2.6 per cent.

That 1.1 per cent a year drop in economic growth suggests that Howard was the better economic manager – especially when combined with the budget surpluses. And that's what you've probably heard from anyone who likes to point back to the 'good old days'.

But context is king, and this is the part you don't often get told/isn't remembered.

Average annual economic growth by Prime Ministership

	Australia	OECD	Difference ▾
Rudd-Gillard	2.64%	0.68%	2.0%
Keating	3.63%	2.60%	1.0%
Albanese	2.08%	1.53%	0.6%
Hawke	3.22%	3.29%	-0.1%
Howard	3.71%	3.87%	-0.2%
Abbott-Turnbull-Morrison	2.37%	2.61%	-0.2%
Fraser	2.58%	3.03%	-0.5%
Whiltam	2.84%	3.31%	-0.5%

Source: Greg Jericho, Chief Economist, The Australia Institute

During Howard's time, economic growth across the OECD averaged 3.9 per cent; during the Rudd–Gillard years, which incorporated the GFC, the OECD average growth was just 0.5 per cent.

Essentially, during the Howard years, Australia's economy grew 0.2 per cent on average slower than the OECD; while during Rudd–Gillard's time in office, Australia's economy grew 1.9 per cent faster than the OECD.

Compared to the OECD, the economy under Howard grew worse than it did under Hawke, Keating, Rudd–Gillard and even the Albanese period to the middle of 2025.

The lesson here is that people believe the story you tell them. Even though the economy underperformed for the time, people still believe Howard and Costello were economic masters. That legacy set the tone for the last three decades. Labor has been hesitant to invest in policies that meet its own platform (higher welfare, investment in social housing, etc) for fear it will be seen as 'wasteful'. Despite the evidence that Labor has managed the economy through tight spots where austerity would have proven to have plunged the country into recession, the myth remains – surplus good, deficits bad.

After winning the 2022 election, Labor immediately set about moderating expectations: it would use its hold over the budget reins to raise people out of poverty, prioritising delivering a surplus. It has been part of a project to try and change people's perceptions over how Labor handles the economy, which is one of the strongest hang-ups from the Howard years.

So, not only do we not get a boldly reformist government, we get one that is still trying to silence the attacks of the past, while dealing with the little budget bombs Howard and co baked into the Budget, that make everything harder than it should be anyway.

The biggest budget timebombs have been in how the Howard years reshaped the tax system.

We know how they screwed us on housing with their tax breaks, but Howard also shifted the balance away from income tax to consumption tax, and in doing so gave the biggest benefits to high income earners – and that remains in place all these years later.

After introducing the GST he promised never to introduce, Howard also sold the furphy that he was going to rebalance the tax system to offset the consumption tax. And while some small changes were made for lower income earners, the bigger gains went to higher income earners.

He raised the top tax threshold from $50,000 in 1999–2000, to $60,000 in 2000–01 and then increased it again to $62,500 in 2003–04 and then $70,000 in 2004–05 to $95,000 in 2005–06 to $150,000 in 2006–07.

Kevin Rudd then continued the trend and pushed it up to $180,000 in 2008–09.

This took the top threshold from just over double median earnings in 2004–05 to four times in 2006–07.

What that means (in non-economist terms), is prior to Howard's changes, the top tax threshold kicked in if you were earning about two times the median wage. After Howard, it kicked in when you were earning about four times the median wage. No government since has ever attempted to return it to a more equitable arrangement, back to where it used to be, for fear of a public lynching.

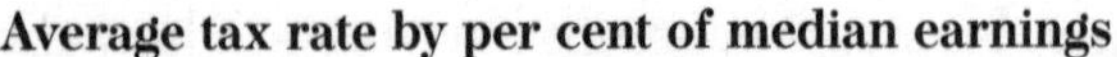

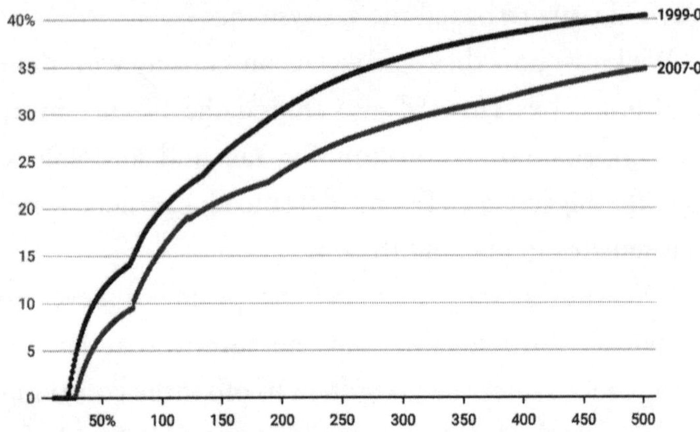

Chart: The Australia Institute. Source: Australian Tax Office and Australian Bureau of Statistics

But prior to Howard, someone earning three times the median wage paid about 17 per cent more income tax. After Howard, that same earner is paying about 12 per cent. But the changes for the lower thresholds were nowhere near as drastic.

The changes Howard did for them didn't do much – it was the Rudd and Gillard governments who addressed that, moving the tax-free threshold from $6000 to $18,200. For context, Howard took the tax-free threshold from $5400 to $6000, while at the same time taking the top tax threshold from $50,000 to $150,000.

The tax system is less fair, certainly less progressive, and because it is politically untenable to raise taxes, it has locked in a flatter tax system than what was in place before he was in power.

Top and second-highest income tax thresholds relative to median earnings

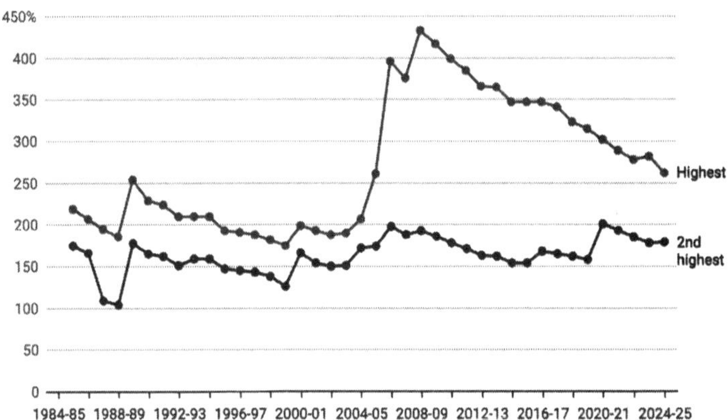

Chart: The Australia Institute. Source: Australian Tax Office

Tax-free thresholds relative to median earnings

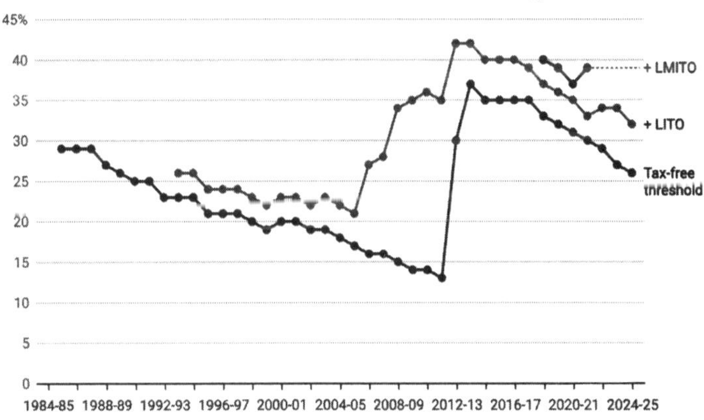

Chart: The Australia Institute. Source: Australian Tax Office

And remember – these tax cuts were paid for by the corporate tax revenue that flowed in during the mining boom, so the moment those receipts stopped coming in at the previous heights, the money had to be found elsewhere. Following the GFC and the implosion of the Labor government, Tony Abbott came to power promising no cuts (having learnt from Howard about core and non-core promises) and then immediately set about trying to slash and burn the Budget.

The Coalition too has been hemmed in by how the Howard years set the tone for the economy – everyone wants tax cuts, but they also want budget surpluses.

We're all obsessed with needing to get debt down, but we're also wondering why no government seems to want to invest in the future.

When it comes to investment, Howard screwed that up too – he and Costello gave birth to the budget trick that was 'funds' with the Future Fund announced in 2004 and legislated in 2006. Instead of spending money, the government takes a headline figure (say $18 billion) and invests it as a sovereign wealth fund. The principal is not used to fund projects and services, but the interest from that principal is. It's a drip feeding of money that makes it seem the government is investing big, when the main investment remains in managing the principal fund itself. Australia now has the DisabilityCare Australia Fund, the Medical Research Future Fund, the Future Drought Fund, the Aboriginal and Torres Strait Islander Land and Sea Future Fund, the Disaster Ready Fund and now the Housing Australia Future Fund.

The problem with the funds is that the people who control them tend to like keeping money in the fund. Which means that it can be difficult for money to be released to pay for what is supposed to be the fund's primary reason for existence. It becomes about keeping the fund strong and growing, rather than prioritising the service or project it was set up to support.

When Labor Treasurer Jim Chalmers asked the fund directors to invest in more housing and green energy, the Coalition and fund guardians lost their minds. Why? Because the fund's primary role is to remain a fund for 'a rainy day', and it doesn't seem to matter how much it is storming out there in reality, the fund must chase financial returns, no matter whether that aligns with Australian values (like when it invests in defence or tobacco stock) or whether the money is needed. When Chalmers changed the fund's direction it had $230 billion in it, from the original $18 billion seed money. It had never been drawn down.

Because why should Australians ever benefit from a fund allegedly set up to benefit Australians when it can just stay in the bank forever growing, never serving?

The little that was given to Australians to compensate for the GST expired, but the tax cuts for the wealthy were baked in (and continue to be). We are taxed how Howard wanted us to be taxed, and we have the mindset Howard wanted us to have.

It was so much easier for him to cut public funding and privatise assets by claiming it was good for the economy. That attitude has remained, but there is never consideration about whether it is good for the people who make up that economy. We are less equal, less supported, less prepared for the future, and the end result has been an ever-widening gap between the rich and the poor that almost seems impossible to bridge.

And we have a Labor Party that rebranded itself as 'economic conservatives' to compete with Howard's myths.

In August 2007, facing the inevitable end of his leadership, Howard stood in parliament and tried to differentiate himself from Rudd who, at that point, was riding unstoppable momentum to the Lodge.

Howard rhetorically asked: if Rudd was no different to him on economic matters, why did Rudd vote against taxation reform (the GST)? Why did he vote against industrial relations reform (WorkChoices)? Why did he vote against tax cuts two Budgets ago (which delivered large cuts to the very richest)? Why did he vote to stop the Budget being put further back into surplus? Why did he vote against the privatisation of Telstra?

In that little bit of rhetoric, Howard finally defined what he believed it meant to be an 'economic radical'; lower taxes for the wealthy, less protections for workers, privatisation of public services, and above all, delivering a surplus, no matter what.

The legacy of that is a media who keep repeating the Howard mantra of 'spend within your means', even if it strangles the future. And all because Howard got lucky.

It's just our bad luck that no one ever seems to be able to look at those years in context.

8
Climate

> 'I've become a climate change agnostic and I think the world is making a mistake by going overboard about climate change. What I mean by that is that I'm not persuaded that the world will come to an end if we don't reduce carbon emissions in a radical way.'[1]
>
> John Howard, September 2025

If there is one issue that shows up the crudeness at the core of John Howard's political instincts, it's the climate.

In the mid-90s, first under Labor and then under Howard and the Coalition, Australia was facing increasing pressure to sign up to international agreements on climate.

Paul Keating and his Cabinet had put in place what was referred to as the 'no regrets' policy, where Australia would not make any pollution concessions that could have any adverse impact on the economy or on trade (oh my, how far we have come!). So, the then–Labor government – in a very tidy full circle moment given the politics of 2020–2025 – was against taxing fossil fuels, with the reasoning that it would increase the cost of power.[2] (Again, this is 1994 and 1995, if you want to feel depressed about how little we have advanced on this.)

In place of any actual action, Keating's Labor government turned to 'carbon sinks' (we just call them carbon credits now), limiting land clearing and planting more trees. Australia had, under Labor, signed up to the Toronto agreement in 1990, which aimed to cut emissions, but only if everyone recognised Australia's reliance on fossil fuels. (Back then the world was hoping we could hold emissions at 1988 levels by 2000 and then cut them by 20 per cent by 2005. HA!)

So, by the time Howard was elected a few years later, the nation was conditioned to not doing a hell of a lot when it came to climate action. That meant Howard didn't have to do much. And he didn't. We knew we would fail to meet the 1990 agreement by 1994, and the next major conference, the Kyoto gathering, wasn't looking too crash hot for Australia, given how little progress we had made.

Howard wasn't too concerned and sent his environment minister, Senator Robert Hill, to Japan to deal with the unpleasantness. At the time, Howard and co viewed Kyoto as a bit of a distraction from some of the domestic political woes he was having. (Too many ministers were failing to meet the ministerial standards, so after having to sack a bunch of them, he lowered the standards rather than improving the ministers.)

Heading into the Kyoto conference, Hill set expectations low:

> It is foolish to believe that we can continue to grow the economy and provide jobs and job security for Australians without there being a resultant effect on energy-related emissions.
>
> The adoption of a uniform reduction target at the upcoming Kyoto conference would have a devastating impact on Australian industry and its ability to create jobs.[3]

In fun news, that media release, from almost three decades ago, includes the line: 'Australia remains a small contributor to total greenhouse gases, contributing only about 1.4 per cent of global emissions.' If that sounds familiar, it's because it has been used by almost every government since to explain why Australia doesn't actually need to be doing more than whatever it is that government has decided to do.

But Hill knew his job, and at the 1997 conference he followed in the spiritual footsteps of Toronto and negotiated Australia a bunch of concessions, including that we could continue to increase emissions.

Howard's first climate plan, 'Safeguarding the Future: Australia's response to Climate Change', released that same year, was pretty much a continuation of the 'no regrets' policy (no regrets, except we killed the planet, soz), with $180 million of new spending over five years, mostly extending existing projects and measures.[4] Reading it now, it's clear it is an early forerunner for the 'technology, not taxes' line the Coalition have been using when it comes to climate policy as recently as the 2025 election.[5] It did, however, establish the mandatory renewable energy target (MRET), which forced electricity retailers and wholesale buyers to collectively achieve a 2 per cent increase in the supply of renewable energy.

But despite winning all those concessions, and changing nothing, Howard refused to ratify the Kyoto agreement, which had the goal of reducing emissions to 5 per cent below 1990 levels between 2008 and 2012 (and then scaling up).

Then there were a few years of back and forth and by 2001 climate action was very unpopular within the Coalition and the Howard Cabinet officially decided not to ratify Kyoto. In 2002 Howard told the parliament, 'It is not in Australia's interests to ratify. The protocol would cost us jobs and damage our industry.'[6] In what is now an age-old trick, Howard claimed that signing up to the Kyoto agreement would create a 'flight of jobs' from the nation's coal sector, as mining companies left Australia to set up in developed nations with less regulation and red tape.

Australia was not alone in not ratifying the agreement – the decision put us in the company of George W. Bush and Vladimir Putin, who had made the same decision for the United States and Russia. (Do you see how little any of this changes yet?)

We can't say that Kyoto didn't do anything, though – it DID help set Australia up for exaggerating our emissions reductions, which we still do today. The 'Australia clause' in the Kyoto Protocol gave Australia the room to include net emissions from land use change when measuring greenhouse gas emissions. This has enabled every government after Howard to claim emissions have been down, even though emissions from actual economic activity have barely fallen.[7] Instead, we just stopped clearing as much land or planted more trees.[8] Emissions have largely not reversed. We simply have the accounting tricks to claim they do. Even with that clause, though, the government refused to ratify the Kyoto Protocol. They got what they needed from it and that was that.

But by 2003 there was pressure to do something; Australia was in the grips of the Millennium Drought, which began with low rainfall in the late 1990s, and by 2003 had been recognised as the worst drought on record. In July of 2003, Peter Costello, Alexander Downer and Joe Hockey were among the Cabinet ministers to make a submission to Cabinet recommending an emissions trading scheme as 'the most cost-effective transition path'.[9] But Howard shut that down very quickly; he gave what the Cabinet papers describe as 'an oral report', but long-time political watchers know that's actually code for a verbal spray – no, his government would not be doing that, thank you very much. The plan was shelved.

In 2004, the same year a plucky, ambitious youngish man named Malcolm Turnbull entered the parliament for the first time, the Howard government released its 'Securing Australia's Energy Future' white paper, which proposed renewable energy initiatives and funding for research and development. In news that would come as no shock to anyone who has ever had anything to do with a white paper, it pretty much reaffirms what the government wants to do anyway, while also declaring that ratifying the Kyoto Protocol isn't in the national interest and it doesn't matter because Australia is on track to meet its targets anyway (we weren't, but thanks to the Australia clause, we could claim we were). In November 2004, Russia ratifies the Kyoto Protocol, but Howard is still claiming it is against Australia's national interest. The country was still in drought, and the longevity of the dry spell, combined with rising concern over major river systems like the Murray–Darling, meant climate awareness was increasing. In 2005, the International Energy Agency reported that Australia's emissions intensity is among the highest in the world and recommends the government consider an emissions trading scheme, which is what Howard's own ministers had suggested in 2003.[10] You know how that went down.

In 2006, *An Inconvenient Truth* was released, a documentary showing former US vice president and failed presidential candidate Al Gore trying to educate people on what was then known as global warming (rather than climate change). It became an ideological brushfire where people, and the politicians who served them, began lining up on either side of the issue. Gore travelled to Australia in September 2006 with the film and Howard refused to meet him, declaring, 'I don't take policy advice from films' (aside from *On the Waterfront*, his favourite film and one he could quote verbatim).[11,12]

Howard's environment minister at that time, Ian Campbell, had just blocked a windfarm from going ahead in Victoria, on the grounds it would pose too great a threat to the critically endangered orange-bellied parrot. The government's own study on the impacts of windfarms on the parrot found it would have 'extremely limited beneficial value to conservation of the parrot without addressing very much greater adverse effects that are currently operating against it', but Howard's government had found a way to use environmental laws, against the environment.[13] (There were just seventeen of the birds left in the wild ten years later in 2016, but the population has recently increased to just over 170, thanks in large part to captive breeding programs. And because nothing is new, in 2025 there are once again concerns about the impact a windfarm, this time in Tasmania, may have on the parrot and its migration flight plan.[14])

That same year, the ABC investigative journalism program *Four Corners* ran a story claiming scientists at the CSIRO were being 'gagged' from disagreeing with the government over its climate policies, which the government denied. (Fresh allegations were raised following Abbott's election in 2013.[15])The CSIRO denied anyone had been gagged, but it also moved away from research into renewable energies, which critics claimed was an attempt to save itself from budget cuts. (In 2014, Abbott cut about $110 million from the CSIRO budget, reducing its workforce by about 20 per cent.[16])

Australia was still in drought. Labor had made believing in climate change and wanting to act on Kyoto a point of difference, and it was taking hold. Not even Howard could hold that tide back, so in December 2006 he announced the government was looking at . . . (wait for it) an emissions trading scheme. He established the Prime Ministerial Task Group on Emissions Trading and asked the group to 'advise on the nature and design of a workable global emissions trading system in which Australia would be able to participate.' He continued, 'The Task Group will advise and report on additional steps that might be taken, in Australia, consistent with the goal of establishing such a system.'[17]

So, Howard went from a 'no thank you, absolutely not, it's not happening', to a 'oh, shit, we are losing the people and we probably should do something, how about that thing we have been rejecting for the last three or so years', just to win an election. It didn't work, and it's been a political plaything ever since, with the Liberal Party choosing to forget it was ever official policy.

One month later, in January 2007, Turnbull was made environment minister, and he began lobbying Howard to ratify Kyoto. Howard didn't publicly bend on that, and the Cabinet rejected a proposal Turnbull put forward to join the agreement, but Howard did appoint Peter Shergold to start designing an emissions trading scheme, which he then took to the 2007 election as Liberal policy.[18,19] The ETS was to start no later than 2012 and its 'long-term aspirational goal' was to reduce carbon emissions.[20] A climate change fund was announced in 2007 (there's always a fund), with revenue from the fund trading to be reinvested into climate change initiatives. Howard went from indifferent, to a sceptic, to a believer, all in the space of eleven years, accelerated in the final term, because he couldn't hide what people had begun to see with their own eyes.

It was all for naught, as Kevin Rudd won the election, ratified Kyoto, set up a climate change department and ministry, started on a carbon pollution reduction scheme (CPRS) and . . . well, we know what happened.[21] The CPRS was delayed and then lapsed (for lots of reasons, but this isn't a book on Labor and the Greens), Rudd was toppled (only marginally related to the CPRS mess), Julia Gillard becomes the leader, winning the support of crossbenchers for a minority government, and agrees to investigate things like a carbon price, passes the carbon price, Tony Abbott labels it a 'carbon tax', and after a lot more mess and back and forth, Abbott wins the 2013 election and one of the first orders of his government is to 'scrap the carbon tax' (it was never a tax). Abbott-era treasurer Joe Hockey gutted the Australian Renewable Energy Agency, described windfarms as 'utterly offensive' and slashed funding in climate-related areas. Abbott was toppled by Turnbull, who was himself toppled by Scott Morrison, after hard-right MPs in his party room rebelled over his National Energy Guarantee policy, which was also designed to cut carbon emissions.[22]

All in all, Australia's climate policy has been a mess since Howard, and even after all that, he maintains no regrets.

From 2008 onwards, Howard was back to his climate sceptic self, declaring in one way or another that he believed the science around climate change to be exaggerated.

In 2008, he first admitted this was based not on science, but his own instinctual beliefs. 'My suspicion is that as time goes by there will be increasing doubts raised in the community about whether everything said in alarmist terms about climate change is correct,' he said.[23]

In 2013 he admitted that the only book he had read on climate change was Nigel Lawson's (a very prominent climate sceptic) *An Appeal to Reason: A Cool Look at Global Warming*, which had been published in 2008.[24]

Just as his protégé Abbott was whirring up to destroy the foundations of Australia's first actual emissions reduction policy, Howard declared:

> I am unconvinced that catastrophe is around the corner. I don't disregard what scientists say. I just don't accept all of the alarmist conclusions. I instinctively feel that some of the claims are exaggerated.

It was that same speech where he said most Australians were with him:

> The high tide of public support for over-zealous action on global warming has passed. My suspicion is that most people in countries like ours have settled into a state of sustained agnosticism on the issue.[25]

In 2013, Howard's answers to Australia's climate ills were backburning and nuclear power.

When discussing a large bushfire that wreaked havoc in Victoria 163 years ago, he said it occurred 'when the planet was not experiencing any global warming. You might well describe all of this as an inconvenient truth.'[26]

Does any of this seem familiar?!

He was still at it in 2022 when he said, 'I think some aspects of the debate have become greatly exaggerated.

Every time there's any kind of disaster it's always put down to climate change. In some cases that's fair and in other cases it's not fair.'[27]

This was after the 2019/20 Black Summer bushfires, by the way. The ones that the Morrison government completely failed to respond to in a way that reassured people their government knew what to do. The Coalition was punished severely in the 2022 election, for a multitude of reasons, but a refusal to form a climate policy chief among them. Blue-ribbon inner-city seats, including those of potential future leaders, were lost by what was called the 'teal wave' with the election of independents, all of whom ran on a platform of climate action, and integrity. As of the 2025 election, the Liberals won only one back but also lost one of their last remaining inner-city seats to another teal independent.

But Howard didn't stop there. Despite going backwards in two elections and experiencing a historic wipe-out in seats – which also cost then-leader, Peter Dutton, his own electorate – Howard was out early urging his party to dump the 'net zero by 2050' goal.

'I've become a climate change agnostic and I think the world is making a mistake by going overboard about climate change,' he said in September 2025.

'What I mean by that is that I'm not persuaded that the world will come to an end if we don't reduce carbon emissions in a radical way.

'I'm doubtful that net zero is worth the price we're paying for it.'

As of writing, the Liberal Party stands on the brink of collapse over the issue, as hard-right MPs have run away with the debate, while the Nationals have threatened to break up the Coalition if the Liberals don't scrap net zero as a policy.

But it is not just the Liberals and the Coalition that have been pulled apart by Howard's refusal to act on climate during government (or even believe in climate change since). Despite what the official government releases might tell you, the data doesn't lie. Australia's greenhouse gas emissions increased during the Howard years and by much more than was projected by the 1997 climate plan. It increased by more than what had been projected in the 'business as usual, do nothing' modelling. His refusal to ratify Kyoto helped shape the next two decades of climate wrecking we have seen from the Coalition following his 2007 election loss and set the groundwork on how to weaponise climate change in Australian politics. Howard, in his 'technology over taxes' early policies, incentivised the private sector and created industries around 'magic tech', which was meant to save us from rising emissions, while ensuring no polluter actually needs to address cutting their emissions. That's still happening, be it through carbon capture abatement or 'technology in the pipeline' that is used to assure the public something will come and save us, while again not doing anything to force big emitters to stop emitting, or indeed, stop opening coal and gas projects.[28]

The government claims Australia has reduced its emissions by 27 per cent compared to the 2005 level, and often uses the figure to claim Australia is on track to meet its climate targets. That's again because of the Howard era, which lets us claim land use even as emissions increase. We still have a massive fossil fuel problem, and by not forcing anyone to deal with it, we have only cut our emissions (compared to 2005 levels) by 3 per cent.[29]

We keep hearing the same lines from the Howard government, even as the need to act grows even more critical. Brian Fisher, an advisor to the Howard government, has spent decades warning of the 'cost' of climate change action, claiming early in the piece that 'early action [on climate] would be more costly than adopting emission pathways with lower near-term mitigation'.[30] It's wrong. Under the brief carbon price period, Australia successfully reduced emissions by 2 per cent while the economy grew by 5 per cent but, at the 2019 election, a report by Fisher was used to detail Labor's climate policy offering during an election campaign that became all about modelling, rather than what might be done and why. His findings were disputed by Labor, as well as a variety of climate and energy experts, but it didn't matter. In 2021, Fisher was hired by the Morrison government to review its latest climate plan, giving climate sceptics further ammunition.[31] His work is still cited by Coalition MPs determined to scrap net zero.

It is not just the economic benefits Howard has cost us, it is the hope that we could act in time, that we could rise above petty politics and act in the interests not just of future generations and at-risk communities – such as those in the Pacific already dealing with the impacts of climate change – but ourselves.

What should have been a no-brainer (that also would have had economic benefits) became an ideological culture war that is still raging today. Both the Coalition and Labor have argued against needing to have a duty of care to future generations included in legislation. Both major parties have mocked school students for daring to protest for their future, and punished protesters old and young for the crime of bringing attention to government inaction. Australia is convinced it needs to keep opening coal and gas mining projects, despite the science telling us we can't afford to. At the core of every reason not to stop coal and gas mining, to actually act on lowering emissions rather than dance around it with claims of future 'technology' that will do it for us, is Howard.

A man still questioning climate change in 2025, even as the world heats up around him.

9
America's Bitch

'My friends, let me say to you today that America has no better friend anywhere in the world than Australia. Australians and Americans enjoy each other's company. We share a love of sport and in some of them we are fierce competitors. And we even from time to time share the Academy Awards.'[1]

John Howard to the US Congress, 2002

In September 2001, John Howard travelled to America to commemorate the fiftieth anniversary of the ANZUS treaty. Signed in 1951 between the United States, Australia and New Zealand, the treaty was part of Australia (and at the time New Zealand) looking for a protector. Following the denuding of Britain after World War II, the fall of Singapore to Japan, the bombing of Darwin and the lack of response from Mother England had Australia and New Zealand looking for a bigger wolf at the door, one that was less focused on Europe.

As the world remapped itself in the wake of World War II, America emerged as a global superpower – and we barnacled ourselves to them.

The treaty is supposed to be about protecting the security in the Pacific, but it was mostly referred to in glowing historic terms of the 'strong' friendship between Australia and the US (New Zealand got itself partially suspended from the treaty in 1986 over a dispute on nuclear weapons).

Howard, ever the lover of history (and the United States), spent four hours on September 10 with George W. Bush, the Republican president, with whom Howard had spent the last year rebuilding Australia's relationship with the US. The first five years of Howard's prime ministership had been spent under Bill Clinton's captaincy of the US, and the pair did not get along. Clinton was frustrated at Australia's churlishness at not wanting to engage on climate issues (something that Bush would then join Howard in), while the US took an Australian leather manufacturer to court, and then later banned Australian and New Zealand lamb exports.[2] In 1997, Australia knocked back (once again) the suggestion of a bilateral free trade deal between the two nations. Relations became fairly frosty from 1999 when the US declined to send troops to Timor-Leste (East Timor), and then privately expressed frustration at Australia's handling of Indonesia and its intelligence over the Timorese massacres.[3] Bush's election win in 2000, despite losing the popular vote to Al Gore and a dispute over which way Florida went, must have been a relief for Howard, and given his own stumbles to power, the pair had a shared appreciation of losing to win. By September 2001, Howard and Bush were close enough that Howard had been invited to address Congress, a big change from his 1999 visit, where he had been lucky to get a terse twenty minutes with Clinton.

Howard stood next to President Bush for a 19-gun salute at a Washington naval dockyard and received the bell from the USS *Canberra* as a gesture of the enduring friendship between the two nations. The USS *Canberra* was already close to Howard's heart – it has been the only US ship commissioned in honour of another nation's lost ship, with president Franklin D. Roosevelt insisting the Baltimore Class Cruiser USS *Pittsburgh* be renamed the *Canberra* after learning of the Australian ship that went down during the Battle of Savo Island. He went to a barbecue with Vice President Dick Cheney, Secretary of State Colin Powell and Secretary of Defense Donald Rumsfeld – the unholy defence trinity of the junior Bush administration.

It's safe to say that as Howard went to sleep on September 10, his heart was full of red, white and blue pageantry and affection.

He woke up on September 11, in a hotel just a few blocks away from the White House in Washington, DC, and was speaking to his press secretary about the coming day's events as the first plane hit the World Trade Center. They thought it was a light aircraft, until the second plane hit the next tower. Howard could hear the sirens from his hotel room as emergency services rushed to the Pentagon, where a third plane had crashed. He could see the smoke rising from his room at the Willard hotel.[4]

From that moment on, whether he knew it consciously or not, Australia was at war with a then still unknown enemy of the US. By then Australian protocols had kicked in and Howard was taken to the basement of the Australian embassy in Washington for safety.

He wrote a letter to Bush that he read out a short time later to Australians in a televised broadcast:

> Dear Mr President. The Australian Government and people share the sense of horror experienced by your nation at today's catastrophic events and the appalling loss of life. I feel the tragedy even more keenly being here in Washington at the moment. In the face of an attack of this magnitude, words are always inadequate in conveying sympathy and support. You can however be assured of Australia's resolute solidarity with the American people at this most tragic time. My personal thoughts and prayers are very much with those left bereaved by these despicable attacks upon the American people and the American nation.[5]

Australia was with America, all the way. We haven't been able to untangle ourselves since.

Howard spent the day after September 11 having high level meetings with American Congress representatives and bureaucrats. He later told Michael Gordon at *The Age* that being in America for September 11 may have led him to commit Australia to America's response faster than he might have, if he had not witnessed the shock firsthand.

'Certainly, being on the spot had a powerful effect on me,' he said.[6]

'I knew how shocked and bewildered the Americans were, although everybody was very calm. Everybody understood that this was a game changer.'

In his autobiography, *Lazarus Rising*, released three years after his electoral defeat, Howard wrote that, as he left the United States, he thought 'we now could be beginning a war on terror that would last for decades'.

He was all in though. As he flew back to Australia on September 12, part of the way on Air Force Two, which the Americans had made available to him, he had a conversation with his minister and ally Alexander Downer, and with history on his mind and the drums of war beating in his heart, he made a historic decision: 'I spoke to Alexander Downer on the phone and out of that conversation the idea of invoking ANZUS came,' he told the *Australian Financial Review* in 2021.[7] He continued:

> I think it was probably Alexander who first said, 'Why don't we invoke ANZUS?' and it seemed on first blush to be the right thing to do, and it seemed to me without having any formal legal advice at that stage, just my own understanding of the fairly simple terms of the treaty, that this was an attack of a metropolitan nature [as stated in Article V of the treaty] on New York and Washington.
>
> It seemed to me to be a symbolic and sensible way of expressing our support to the Americans at a very difficult time.[8]

Two days later, Howard held a press conference with Downer and announced, for the first, and only time since, the ANZUS treaty was officially invoked.

What did it mean?

Article IV of ANZUS says that an attack on one of the parties would create a 'common danger' for all parties, and that they will 'act' to meet that threat to their shared peace and safety. 'If ANZUS is meant to cover a situation, surely it covers this,' Howard announced.

It is highly debatable that America would ever come to Australia's rescue, if the need arose, if it were not heavily in America's own interest. So it makes complete sense that it would be Howard's Australia which invoked the treaty, coming as it did on the heels of all the work Howard had done to revive the Anzac legend to the point of jingoistic suffocation.

Unlike the Nato agreement, the ANZUS treaty doesn't mean diddly squat in terms of guarantees. It's more of a feel-good statement of vibes and maybes, despite what the Americancultists might claim.

The upshot of it all was that Australia would officially consider any requests from the United States for help, should they come. They did, not long after, and when Bush announced America was going to war 'on terror' in October 2001, Howard had already committed Australia to following.

That decision re-shackled Australia to America's foreign policy and became the longest foreign war of our history.

Dr Emma Shortis, in her 2021 book *Our Exceptional Friend: Australia's Broken Relationship with America*, notes the decision as the one that has kept us chained to the US for strategic, defence and foreign policy ever since: 'Once Howard had got Australia in, there was apparently no way out.'

In 2011, a decade on from the September 11 attacks, Australians were still fighting the war Howard had committed them to. There were still no clear mission goals, or even an idea of what success would look like. Then–prime minister Julia Gillard told the nation that while the cost of the war had been bitter, we needed 'to see the mission through'. Not even Howard could identify success as he did media for the tenth anniversary of September 11: 'It's not something that has a defined date when you can declare victory,' he told Gordon in 2011.[9] 'It's not like a conventional war, where eventually one side unconditionally surrenders, as the Germans and the Japanese did in World War II.'

No one surrendered, although the US did eventually give up its latest never-ending war in 2021, which gave Australia permission to call all its ADF back.

The Department of Veterans' Affairs reports about 40,000 ADF personnel served in Afghanistan operations between 2001 and 2021, when the last of the 'Coalition of the Willing' troops withdrew, leaving Afghanistan back at the mercy of the Taliban. Forty-seven Australians paid the ultimate price on the battlefields. Twenty-six were wounded. The unseen wounds many came home with were documented in the royal commission into veteran suicide. Australian soldiers were, as of late 2025, still under investigation for alleged war crimes committed against Afghanistan citizens.

In 2003, Bush honoured Howard with the Presidential Medal of Freedom for being his 'man of steel' who never wavered in his support of the US campaign.

At the time, Howard was still convinced the invasion would go down as a Western success, and he could live out his Anzac dream of being a victorious wartime prime minister.

'I think the military textbooks will be replete with the experiences of Operation Iraqi Freedom for many years to come,' he said at the ceremony where he was given the US's highest civilian honour.[10]

'The leadership of the US, with the support of its coalition partners, Great Britain, Australia, Poland and others, I think has sent a very important message, not only to the region, but also to the rest of the world.'

He was right, but not for the reasons he had thought at the time.

We know now that not only was the invasion and resulting war a resounding failure for the US and the allies that followed it in, it was ultimately pointless and the evidence suggests it has actually made the world *less* safe, by fostering the origins of terrorist groups such as Islamic State.

The US 'shock and awe' Iraq invasion in 2003 may have cost up to one million Iraqis their lives, and hinged on a widely disputed report that then-leader Saddam Hussein had been stockpiling weapons of mass destruction, as well as a nuclear program. Despite UN weapons inspectors finding no evidence to support the US and UK claims Hussein was stockpiling 'weapons of mass destruction' and planned to make more in early 2003, the US, the UK and Australia were all in and invaded just a couple of months after the UN report.[11] By 2004, it was clear the reports were false.[12]

Insert Howard's gasp face.

'I felt embarrassed, I did, I couldn't believe it, because I had genuinely believed it,' he said in a 2014 interview.[13]

'So, I felt embarrassed and I did my best to explain . . . that it wasn't a deliberate deception. It may have been an erroneous conclusion based on the available information, but it wasn't made up.'

Howard believed the claims so strongly that he sent Australia to war with just an oral submission to the Cabinet in 2003. The decision sent hundreds of thousands of people into the streets in February 2003, a month before the formal decision, in what was then one of the biggest national protests ever seen. The then–Labor opposition leader, Simon Crean, called the invasion decision 'a black day for Australia'. Andrew Wilkie, who later became an independent MP, resigned from the Office of National Assessments in protest. The Cabinet papers released show there was barely any discussion of the decision, with most of the calls seemingly made in the National Security Committee (NSC) – a secretive committee Howard set up in 1996 to sit inside but separate to Cabinet, to limit transparency even further.[14]

Howard, who in 2002 had declared the United States 'has no better friend anywhere in the world' and who had accepted the 'deputy sheriff' moniker from Bush (despite the unease it caused with Australia's Muslim neighbours in the Pacific) had committed Australia to an open-ended war, with no goals in sight, without even requesting any advice on the pros or cons of the decision. The public service, well aware of the situation, did not offer any advice that either supported or cautioned against the decision. There was no cost–benefit analysis. The UN Security Council had not explicitly signed off on the decision, so Howard relied on a 'Memorandum of advice to the Commonwealth government on the use of force against Iraq' from two junior bureaucrats to assure the public that Australia's involvement in the invasion of Iraq was 'legal'.[15]

When the Governor-General at the time, Peter Hollingworth, had asked to see legal advice from Attorney-General, Daryl Williams, on Australia's involvement under international law, given the longstanding precedent that it was the Governor-General who declared war, he was told there was no need.

Instead, Howard used a clause in the Defence Act that gave the defence minister the power to give instructions to the heads of service.[16]

All so he could be all the way with the US and strengthen an alliance with the country he had admired since childhood. In the early stages of Australia's involvement in the US's war, Howard also approached the US over signing a bilateral free trade deal, which, as Emeritus Professor of Politics Robert Manne pointed out, Australia had previously rejected three times, including under Howard, as not being in the national interest. So eager at this point, or perhaps wildly miscalculating Washington's actual gratitude at Australia's subservience, Australia ended up with a deal that was, shockingly, not in the national interest.

We have never rebalanced the scales. Not even Labor dare criticise or distance Australia from the US, not in strategic and defence policy, and not in foreign policy, even as it becomes increasingly authoritarian and anti-democratic. Labor had stood against Australia's entry into America's war (while still supporting the ADF), but by the time a young Mark Latham described the Howard government as a 'conga line of suckholes' desperate for the approval of 'the most incompetent and dangerous president in living memory' in 2003, the relationship between the US and Australia was so enmeshed that the US ambassador to Australia at the time complained.[17] Latham was denounced in the Australian media for a lack of civility, and so began Labor's cowing on the US question.[18] Latham was elected Labor leader less than a year after the controversy. He held a press conference shortly after with a US flag in the backdrop and very quickly declared, 'I believe in the American alliance.'[19]

We still believe in the American alliance. No matter what, no matter who. Australia has signed up to deliver at least $360 billion in a strategic defence deal with the United States and the United Kingdom, in the hopes of receiving nuclear-powered submarines from the US that they are under no obligation to deliver.

Even as Donald Trump carries out extrajudicial killings, sacks public servants who try to uphold the law, goes after the judiciary, targets political opponents for retribution, uses his public office for personal wealth building, encourages the kidnapping of people from US streets, unloads tariffs on allied nations, sparks trade wars, insults world leaders and allies, starves his citizens, guts public services and spending, pushes for gerrymanders, declares himself a king and above the law, lies, appoints reality TV stars and cronies to senior ministerial roles, and openly discusses a third term, Constitution be damned, Australia is by his side. Literally. At a dinner held for APEC leaders in South Korea in late 2025, Albanese was sat at Trump's side. His 'right hand man' as it were.

It doesn't matter that America's democracy is crumbling as it projects its political violence outwards in its attempts to violently rebuild its 'empire', or that the 'shared values' Australian leaders have long claimed we and the United States have in common are more nostalgic than reality – Australia is in lockstep with the US. Howard tied us to America so tightly, it would take a world-altering event to unshackle us. The tragic truth is though, even then, we would probably be on America's side, even if it meant our own destruction.

10

IR and Wages

> 'I mean, these are not the battlers of the trade union movement. Many of them earn $100,000 a year. They are not battlers. They are the elite of the trade union movement and they have privileges that battlers in the trade union movement elsewhere in Australia don't have. And we want lower costs on the wharves so our exporters can do more business overseas and employ more Australians. Now that is what it is all about.'[1]
>
> John Howard on the waterfront dispute, 1998

In 1998, John Howard went on the very popular Kerri-Anne Kennerley *Midday* show and gave away an actual piece of himself.

One of the ways Howard proved his ordinary bona fides was to go on the shows the ordinary people watched. He did the very serious interviews his predecessors frequented, and spoke to all media outlets, no matter their ideological bent, because he knew the secret to his long-term success was in reaching audiences who did not yet stand with him. That meant showing up on housewife and retiree favourites, as well as the heavy hitters.

In 1998, Howard was still in the early stages of what would be his long-term project of stealing away a percentage of Labor's voter base. He didn't need all of them, just enough of them. He'd had some success by letting Pauline Hanson run free saying all the things he couldn't say (but didn't mind being said). He would continue to build on that success his entire leadership career, and beyond – he still attempts to present himself as the voice of 'ordinary, quiet Australians', even as the linear nature of time picks away at his relevancy.

Having campaigned strongly on industrial relations reform at the 1996 election (which was one of the reasons he had entered politics in the first place), Howard had already enacted some legislation, including the *Workplace Relations Act 1996*, which restricted the operation of the Australian Industrial Relations Commission to twenty 'allowable award matters' and narrowed the scope for arbitration. Unions had their power gutted further by the introduction of Australian workplace agreements – individual written agreements on terms and conditions between employer and employee, rather than collective bargaining. The legislation also outlawed closed shops (where the employer must hire union members and employees must remain members of the union while employed) and restricting union activities (such as strike action) by giving employers more legal rights to counter industrial action.

Under Howard, the vernacular started to change too; union leaders became 'union bosses', and actual bosses in private enterprise, became 'business leaders'.

At the time of his election, the strongest unions in Australia covered the wharves, coal mining, the building industry and the meat processing industry.

It didn't hurt that Howard's right-hand man was Peter Costello, who in the mid-1980s had helped form the H.R. Nicholls Society, which was created with the intention of overhauling Australia's arbitration and centralised wage fixing system.[2] As a lawyer, pre-politics, Costello had made his name representing employers in their legal battles with Australian unions. He was well up for the challenge of gutting the power of Australian unions and set to work almost as soon as the last ballot was counted in the 1996 election. Of course, the unions protested (which was what Howard wanted) and about 20,000 union members and supporters descended on Parliament House in Canberra on August 20, 1996, and during the speeches a small group broke away and began storming inside.

Iron stakes, sledgehammers and battering rams were used to break through the 300-strong police line guarding the doors; the foyer was left bloody, the gift shop trashed, and by the time police had managed to repel the group two hours later, seventy of the 300 police were injured along with protesters, forty-nine of whom were arrested.

Despite attempts to distance themselves from the violence, both Labor leader Kim Beazley and union leaders had been damaged by the event and Howard seized on it, using it to wield the term 'un-Australian' for one of the first times since becoming prime minister and vowing his government would not take a backwards step: 'I don't believe for a moment that those people who smashed their way into Parliament House in any way represent the feelings of mainstream Australia. I think what they did this afternoon will be greeted with revulsion by mainstream Australia,' he said immediately after.[3]

Howard had his culture war and his excuse, and he gleefully turned to the Maritime Union of Australia (MUA).

By the time he was sitting with Kerri-Anne Kennerley on the *Midday* couch in 1998, the waterfront dispute was well underway, and Howard and the managing director of Patrick Stevedores, Chris Corrigan, had made it very clear they wanted to completely overhaul work practices on the docks. The ban on closed shops had opened the wharves up to non-unionised labour, the National Farmers' Federation was on board with the private stevedores to smash up the union hold on ports, and Howard's job was a full-frontal public soothing.[4] It wasn't about smashing unions, goodness no! It was all about lowering prices for Australians by creating some competition on the docks, that was all!

Speaking to Kennerley, Howard said:

> The purpose of this is one thing and one thing alone, and that is to generate more jobs for Australians. The reason we want a better waterfront is not to bash up a union, that's not the purpose. I have got no argument with unions as such, I just want a more efficient waterfront.
>
> I mean we changed the law to allow non-union labour onto the waterfront and we have now got a farmer-owned company that is going into business and going into competition with existing stevedores. Now that is terrific. It is like anybody opening up a new business and if they can provide competition, get the prices down, we all benefit and there are more jobs.[5]

He then revealed that not only was *On the Waterfront* – the Elia Kazan, Marlon Brando classic about union violence and corruption in New Jersey his favourite film, he could quote it, verbatim, cutting off Kennerley as she started with '"I could have been a contender—"'

'"I could have gone somewhere, I could have been something and you said no we are going for a price on Wilson and I had to take a dive", that's what he said. It was a great movie,' Howard interrupted.

It is unclear whether the man who admitted to loving Bob Dylan and Joan Baez for their voices and not their lyrics knew that Kazan had made the film after he gave up eight names to the 1950s House Committee on Un-American Activities, as an explanation of sorts, but it didn't matter. Howard knew your favourite movies, middle-aged Australia, and he was casting himself as Brando, trying to stand up to the big, powerful, immoral unions.

After a series of extraordinary events that involved Patrick Stevedores taking control of the docks, boats being deployed in the middle of the night, and locking out and firing 1400 union workers, the MUA retained the right to represent waterfront workers, but only after hundreds of redundancies and longer hours for lower pay.[6]

Howard had broken the back of one of Australia's most powerful unions and undermined union power in just two years of governing. His job had been made easier by the Hawke and Keating Accords, which had neutered the unions' wage demands in return for public services like Medicare. Labor had, once again, made the mistake of not considering what would happen with their laws and policies when they weren't in power (a mistake Labor has continued to make), and someone with more iniquitous intentions held the reins.

Howard continued waging his war of attrition against the unions, utilising the python squeeze strategy, rather than the taipan strike. Over time, Howard made it harder to organise, harder to strike and harder to form a collective. He changed tax law to give tradespeople an incentive to become self-employed contractors rather than employees (come on down Morrison's tradies), and much like his media strategy of shearing off some of Labor's base, he also pursued the working-class ute drivers with the same zeal he used to gain the coveted pensioner vote. He squeezed the unions by making their life harder while peeling off categories of workers, mostly men, from the Labor Party. Unions lost membership fees and members, which then reduced what could be donated to the Labor Party, impacting Labor's spend at elections. But it also neutered how hard unions themselves could go after Howard without risking the loss of further members and supporters to Howard's tune.

At every election, Howard would warn of the return of union dominion under a Labor government (never mind it was Labor policies that had laid the foundation for all Howard wanted and did to undermine union power). Thanks to Howard taking all of Labor's reforms and going even further to screw over workers, solidarity and sympathy strike action is banned, enterprise agreements are now entrenched in Australian workplaces, and it is the employer who controls how they are created, resulting in the stagnation of wages and conditions.

But it wasn't just workplace or tax legislation that Howard utilised – he was also a big fan of using free trade deals to undercut Australian workers. Historically, it has been difficult for Labor/Labour governments to do bilateral trade agreements, partly because it lessens control over migration numbers, but mostly because it would mean sacrificing trade protections that protect jobs. Howard had no such qualms, as sacrificing jobs in the manufacturing industry meant less unionised workers and a weaker union, usually in exchange for protecting the (very lightly unionised) agricultural sector, which made the junior Coalition partner, the Nationals, happy.

Tony Abbott took those lessons to heart, with his government in 2014 goading the car manufacturing industry to leave Australian shores – so gleeful were they to deliver another blow to the Australian Workers Union. (They were so obsessed with continuing Howard and Costello's mission that the act of bastardry that ultimately damaged the Liberals worse didn't appear to be properly considered at the time.)

Howard made being the son of a petrol station owner part of his 'ordinary' log cabin story, and used it to keep squeezing unions. Individual contracts helped undercut pattern bargaining (when a union wins a favourable agreement at one employer and then uses it as the model for agreements at others) and he did it while always claiming he wasn't against unions, he was just for business and choice. He didn't hate unions! He just hated what they did.

While Howard was very successful in radically reforming industrial relations, he was still held back by the Senate from doing every aspect of his plan and was at the mercy of negotiating with the Democrats and others to pass the legislation Labor opposed.

Then came 2004, when thanks to One Nation preferences, Queensland Senate results delivered Howard three Liberals and one National senator – Barnaby Joyce (just one of the long-term benefits Howard received from never directly challenging Hanson and One Nation). Labor won the remaining two, but Joyce's unlikely victory gave Howard thirty-nine seats in a seventy-six seat Senate – the first time a government had dominance over the parliament since the Fraser government in the 1970s. Queensland veteran Nationals Senator Ron Boswell literally cried as the results became clear and called Howard to personally deliver the news that he had control over the legislative agenda.

'The prime minister has said he is not going to abuse the power and he is going to be very careful what he puts through,' Boswell said with a straight face shortly after the election.[7]

After eight years of the python squeeze, Howard then went for the taipan strike with WorkChoices. He passed it in December 2005, and by 2006 it began hitting workplaces. His legislation removed the 'no disadvantage' test that had previously applied to individual workplace agreements (AWAs) and meant that an individual agreement could not be worse than the relevant award that applied to the sector. It was a safety net for employees not covered by the award and limited the power of employers to strip workers of rights. Even so, before the removal of the test, employees on AWAs tended to be worse off than those covered by the awards. When the government scrapped the test, there was nothing stopping employers to force a 'take it or leave it' AWA on their employees, which in most cases was worse than the award they had previously been covered by.[8]

WorkChoices also superseded state powers over industrial relations that created a single national system covering about 85 per cent of workers.[9] Penalties for unlawful strikes and industrial action increased, businesses with less than a hundred employees became exempt from unfair dismissal laws and employment contracts and agreements only needed to meet five basic minimum standards: the minimums on wages, annual leave, personal leave, parental leave and working hours.

Howard had achieved his lifelong political dream of handing power to employers and tearing down union power in the workplace. The taipan strike finished what he had started, but it also galvanised unions in a way not seen since the 1970s. Arguably, you could say Work-Choices ultimately sowed the seeds of union movement restoration and the Your Rights at Work campaign was the start of the resurgence. With Kevin Rudd appearing young(ish) and fresh in comparison to Howard, promising new ideas (even if there was no real strategy for implementing them), vowing to be an 'economic conservative' so as not to spook those sick of Howard but still wary of Labor, and the ACTU-led campaign against WorkChoices, Howard was all but done.[10]

The 2007 election (which up until months before, the senior members of the federal press gallery were convinced Howard would win and were writing as such) saw Kevin from Queensland rise to power and Howard became just the second prime minister since Federation to lose his own seat at an election. He would still say it was worth it.

Union membership had dropped from 2.19 million in 1996 when Howard was elected and sat at around 1.69 million by the time he left in 2007, when just 19 per cent of the workforce was unionised. The number of self-employed people grew from 1.67 million in 1998 to 2.03 million a decade later.[11]

As with everything else, the industrial relations landscape Howard left was very different from the one he took over.

Rudd repealed part of WorkChoices in 2009 and replaced it with the *Fair Work Act 2009*, which remains the foundation of today's industrial relations legislation. But it didn't give workers back all the power that had been stripped away. The *Fair Work Act* retained the main restrictions on strike actions and retained the national system for workplace relations that WorkChoices had established through the National Employment Standards (although the *Fair Work Act* was achieved through negotiations with the states, rather than imposed like WorkChoices). The NES included ten minimum standards compared to WorkChoices' five, adding in public holidays, annual leave, long service leave, work hours, flexible work arrangement requests and boundaries over notice of termination. These have been expanded over time. But while the *Fair Work Act* banned further adoption of AWAs, it continued the fundamental shift from the traditional collective bargaining model, and employers retain control over the agreement-making process with employees in most industries, rather than collective bargaining (although the Albanese government did move to give some industries, including those in the care sector, better collective bargaining powers).

The 'no-disadvantage test' was replaced with the 'better off overall test' (BOOT), which applied to 122 'modern' awards and meant workers had to be better off overall, rather than just not worse (which gave Liberals who came after Howard something to focus on destroying).

Howard lost the election but achieved his life's work. He calculated that Labor would be reluctant to undo most of that 'achievement', and he was right. The ACTU had to wait until Anthony Albanese and Tony Burke were elected about fifteen years later to put in place things like multi-employer bargaining that gave unions power to bargain on behalf of employees. The change was almost immediate – average annualised wages grew by their highest rate since 1997 in the December 2024 quarter, with an average pay rise of 4.8 per cent.[12]

But as of August 2024, of the 12.1 million employees in the workforce, just 1.6 million or 13.1 per cent were members of a union. That was up from August 2022 when it was 12.5 per cent and is still the first increase in union membership since 2011. But in 1992, the proportion of the workforce that belonged to a union was 40 per cent.

You can, however, thank Howard for changing the face of union membership. As much as the Coalition still like to paint union members as 'thugs' and paint pictures of scary CFMEU members terrorising construction sites, women outnumber men in the union movement, and professionals and community and personal service workers make up 36 per cent of the union's strength, compared to 16 per cent in the more traditional union areas of machinery operators and drivers.

Women had always been Howard's blind spot, and he used the tax system and every other lever he could to discourage women from entering the workforce (family tax benefit, etc). The Liberals have always opposed free, universal childcare (although tax deductible nannies for the wealthy is acceptable), which has been one of their biggest blind spots in boosting both labour force participation and GDP.

But the combination of the population growth Howard loved (one for mum, one for dad and one for the country!) increasing demand for health care from the aging baby boomers Howard derived a lot of his power from, and the expectation that rich nations provide high-quality health and aged care, have driven demand for care work, which is still heavily unionised. Hospitals are huge, concentrated workforces where it is comparatively easy to encourage union participation. The aged care and early childhood education sector is not as easy as a hospital, but it's still easier than residential construction or small manufacturing, where employers, or self-employed contractors still dominate.

The ACTU put women at the front of the 'Your Rights at Work' campaign, led by then-president Sharan Burrow, and it's continued with Sally McManus and Michele O'Neil who continue to show women around the nation that the union movement is for them.

But still, Howard did lasting damage. The Coalition's deliberate policy of wage stagnation, combined with gutting union power between 2012 and 2022, has been estimated by researchers at Per Capita to have lowered the average yearly wage by almost $12,000 compared to what it would have been if wage growth had kept up with the historical average over that period.[13] It has also impacted the housing crisis, as millennials and gen Z had less chance of saving for a deposit than their parents at the same age. Student unionism was completely crushed and has never recovered. Union membership in the public sector remains low.[14] Workers will likely never regain any more protections than they currently hold, with Labor still unwilling to use its own power to completely reinstate what Howard took away.

Howard didn't just want to defeat Labor, he wanted to dismantle the entire labour movement.

And in some ways, he succeeded, or at least permanently weakened, its power by turning acceptance of the collective into the power of the individual. Tax reform is harder because tax became a personal enemy, rather than a social necessity to better enrich us all. Howard's battlers turned on those they saw as getting something for nothing (people on welfare), middle-class welfare through tax subsidies became entrenched, protest and strike action is considered, at best, an inconvenience rather than a collective show of will to improve a situation, and we've spent the past three decades undervaluing workers and lauding capital, clearing the way for unregulated tech industries and advancements, such as artificial intelligence, to almost seem inevitable.

Howard used his power, flew very close to the sun, and while he may have crashed back down to earth, workers retain the scorch marks.

11
The Liberal Party

> 'I would describe myself as an economic liberal, although, albeit self-confessedly, a bit of a social conservative.'[1]
>
> John Howard, November 1996

Contrary to the rewritten history that paints John Howard as the Grand Poobah of the Liberal Party, a man so respected that the raise of a bushy eyebrow is all it takes to change the party's course, Howard spent most of his time in the Liberal Party being actively despised.

Prior to regaining the leadership after Alexander Downer's spectacular own-goal destruction (look up 'things that batter' for a refresh), Howard was known within the Liberals as 'the rat'. The kind explanation was because he spent his political career 'gnawing' at his leaders, the other, a little more explicit. His reputation was enough that when faced with finding a new leader after John Hewson lost the unlosable election and the choice was between Howard and Alexander Downer, they (without question) went with Downer.

Downer crashed and burned, and Howard became the last man standing – but he still had to spend a lot of time convincing colleagues that he had changed from the man they had dumped five years before and he could be born again into someone less . . . Howard of the last two or so decades. Howard was born again for the 1996 election. He loved Medicare, he was never going to embrace a GST, he was wrong to have criticised Asian migration and, most importantly, at least to his then-colleagues, he embraced the Liberal tradition of a 'broad church' and accepted that they needed to embrace both conservatives and liberals for the party to work. What was Howard? He was both and neither, and something else entirely. And after winning the 1996 election, not on a wave of personal popularity, but on the tsunami of Paul Keating's unpopularity, Howard told the Centre of Independent Studies just that:

> We've had a lot of debate over the last couple of years about whether so-called economic rationalism has gone too far and I think I'm the first speaker to dare utter those two words tonight. I mean, if you were looking for a generic term to describe all of us, a lot of people out there would say that we were sort of economic rationalists and

a lot of you might think others are more sort of economic rationalists than you individually might be. We would describe ourselves perhaps differently. I would describe myself as an economic liberal although albeit self-confessedly a bit of a social conservative. Others would describe themselves by some other label but whatever it is I think we have a rough understanding that we have certain threads in common and those threads in common consist of profound scepticism that Governments can solve all of our problems. I think that's the first thing that we have in common. We have a passionate belief in individual self-fulfilment and achievement. I think we all have a passionate belief that a sense of civic responsibility and a view that we ought to care for people and not in some kind of patronising way or suffocating way but in a sense of civic responsibility and I think finally we also have as people I think as a sense that you do need cohesive units and stabilisers in our society and the greatest stabiliser of all still for all its imperfections is the family unit, and I would like to think that the bonds that bind us together, let's not have a simplistic slogan of economic rationalist or this or that. Some of us in different ways may find those terms offensive, but perhaps those four things bind us together in a very very powerful way.[2]

Australia was still getting to know the slightly strange, very ordinary, bumbling, quiet conservative they had been told they had elected, but a shift was underway within the Liberal Party.

And it's been screwed ever since.

The inevitable end point of John Howard's stewardship of the Liberal Party is the empty vessel we see today. Having gone backwards in two elections, it continues to dig down as the spiritual successors to Howard's leadership continue to drive the party into the abyss. After the 2025 election, the Liberal Party was reduced to a historic low of 29 per cent representation in the House of Representatives and as at the end of 2025, were doing their level best to drop that even further. It has no direction, no centre, no sense of identity beyond the individual desires of the loudest voices concerned with their own worldview, the electorates be damned. Howard has been forced to increasingly intervene, both publicly and privately, to caution the party over tearing itself apart over culture wars – or attempting to import culture wars from the polarised US and UK. It was like a zookeeper teaching his monkeys how to light a fire and then getting shocked when they burn the zoo down.

So how did we get here?

Well, like everything else Howard did, it wasn't overnight. It was a deliberate and consistent death by a thousand cuts until it was just the new normal.

He managed to convince everyone he was supportive of the 'broad church' because he supported the wets sometimes and the dries others, but what no one seemed to notice was that it had to be when it suited him, or else he just didn't care about the issue. Howard was resolute on some things, flexible on others, but no one got everything they wanted – except, well, Howard.

Having experienced political defeat and life in the political wilderness, Howard was astute and focused on how to stay in control of his internal politics, just as much as he was to win elections. It was never a given that Howard was wildly popular with the electorate, or that he would win the next election, but even as polls worried his Cabinet, he was never challenged. Peter Costello was the perfect 'heir apparent' and walked around with the Kirribilli agreement in his wallet (where Howard agreed to retire and transition power to Costello), but his entitlement fooled him into believing power was something given to you. Howard always knew it was something to take. He was so obsessively secretive about his future plans that he told ABC News Radio's Marius Benson that when he had thoughts about his future, he wouldn't even write them down as diary entries.[3]

So how did Howard maintain power for eleven years, even as it became clear rot was setting in? Much like a Labor factional deal, Howard made sure everyone got something. The economic liberals got their IR and tax policies, and the social conservatives got their culture wars about gay marriage/abortion/the family unit.

At the same time, Howard simultaneously made those groups fear each other. He told the liberals that the social conservatives were a bit worried about being so nasty to the poor and he told the conservatives that Costello and the other wets were on the march on the republic, climate change and same sex marriage. Everyone got something, but they feared losing it in battles within their own party, and Howard spent his time as leader sitting at the top, deciding which scale pan to drop a banana in. He knew that to keep his monkeys fighting each other, and not him, he had to keep things balanced at times and uncertain at others.

One of his most effective ways, learned from having been a victim of it under Malcolm Fraser, was to always make sure his rivals were fighting each other. So first it was Costello versus Peter Reith. Once Costello vanquished Reith, he then had to face Tony Abbott. Then Malcolm Turnbull. Costello was battling Howard's various favourites to retain his position as the heir apparent, while Howard's favourites were also busy battling each other to one up each other in the pecking order.

Those who could see through those tricks, like Philip Ruddock (and later George Brandis), who were motivated by core liberal beliefs, were tied up in other ways. Ruddock was once an Amnesty International badge-wearing floor crosser. Howard made him Immigration

Minister, elevated him to Cabinet and made him the face of demonising refugees. Ruddock was silenced.

And while Howard held the power, Costello held the treasury and, in the absence of power, enjoyed telling backbenchers and ministers they couldn't have projects or policies funded. All it did was make Howard safer. Costello never came close to having the numbers needed to pull off a coup, even if he ever did feel brave enough to challenge Howard.

The culture wars Howard promoted worked in dividing the nation and creating the 'us' and 'them' he wanted, but it also alienated broad sectors of new voters. According to the AEC, 25 per cent of voters at the 2025 election were aged eighteen to thirty-four.

All they have ever known of the Liberal Party is what Howard set up: a group of culture war loving, women and minority disparaging, public service gutting, climate sceptics. The 2025 election was the first where millennials and gen Zs toppled the baby boomer dominance in population numbers. The tax, housing and social systems Howard set up to keep the baby boomers 'relaxed and comfortable' have left their children and grandchildren stressed and anxious. The party he moulded in his own image has been unable to move on from the strategies he used to maintain power three decades ago. Howard wanted women in the home, and the Liberal Party, which had always been seen as the party for women, began losing women voters. That was compounded by Howard's favourite of the favourites, Tony Abbott, who made himself the Minister for Women after telling women that supporting climate change action would make their power bills go up every time they turned the iron on. Howard didn't support quotas for improving the number of women in the Liberal Party (and still doesn't, arguing for the imaginary 'merit'), so the Liberal Party doesn't support quotas. No matter that there are now more independent 'teal' women MPs than Liberal women in the House of Representatives, Howard did not and does not believe gender equality equals electoral success, and therefore, the party won't even attempt it. Not that it matters now. It's too late.

Howard had leveraged the discomfort with the social justice changes Paul Keating had been pushing to win power, but the party never moved on. He papered over the structural problems emerging in the party (as demographics and societal attitudes began to shift in the later 2000s) by weaponising racism, pretending the mining boom was sound economic management, and that a population being priced out of rentals was a sign of growing wealth for all. He was helped by Labor continuing to shoot itself in the foot with its choice of leader and confused policy agenda, much because the party didn't (and still doesn't) know how to make its arguments in the Australia Howard created. But now, all those chickens are coming home to roost.

The Liberals were never a broad church. But Howard managed to use a very narrow agenda to appeal to a broad voter base. He used individual desires, aspiration and jealousy (with a healthy dose of racism) to do it, but that appeal has dulled thirty years later. Abbott finishes his telling of the history of Australia with the loss of the Voice referendum, which almost seems the final bookend to Howard's style of politics. Abbott knew how to say no and wreck things thanks to coming up through the Liberal Party in Howard's shadow. But he wasn't ordinary enough to see his culture wars and identity politics as a leader succeed. His credibility only remains because he was booted as leader before he could truly disappoint everyone with his inability to not only lead, but read a room. Those after Howard had learned the lesson about seizing power, but not what to do with it. Abbott was great at being a wrecker, but he had no clear vision of what he wanted to achieve as prime minister and, by then, was firmly entrenched in governing for the front pages of the Murdoch newspapers and its *Sky After Dark* crew. His greatest achievement was helping to sow the seeds that led to Malcolm Turnbull's political demise. For many in the party, that is enough.

Turnbull's toppling (after he attempted to establish an energy and emissions reduction policy) proves the Liberals are not a broad church. Moderate Liberals are allowed to raise concerns about policy, but are never actually allowed to enact it.

Howard set up his power base by allowing the Nationals to capture the parts of One Nation they could and share the dividends among the Coalition more broadly (One Nation preferences in 2004 almost went fifty-fifty between the third Liberal Senate candidate and Nationals' Barnaby Joyce). Howard gave Joyce credibility and helped establish him on the national stage, where, under Abbott, the unearned reputation of 'Australia's best retail politician' was spread until it just became something people said as fact.

With the rise of Joyce came the rise of the Nationals as arbitrators of Liberal policy. Howard had let them run, Abbott let them run, and Morrison let them riot. As the Nationals cost the Liberals more and more seats, the Nationals' voice only gets louder in the Coalition. In 2025, the party formally decided to reject net zero by 2050, despite it being electoral poison for the Liberals, and indeed, the Nats. Joyce declared to all and sundry, as he openly flirted with the possibility of officially becoming a member of One Nation, that he doesn't care if it costs them an election – scrapping net zero is what he believes needs to be done. The Nationals' thirty-year battle defending themselves against One Nation has made it impossible for the Liberals to defend themselves against the Greens and independents.

Labor has managed to sit back and ride the wave, having taken up much of the centre right policy space the Liberals once claim to service. The states crumbled first – branch stacking and the rise of evangelicals in Liberal heartland led to the parties becoming basket cases in Victoria, the ACT and Western Australia. New South Wales looks like following suit and Queensland is only being held together by the memory of its own wipe-out loss in 2015. It's already showing signs of cracking. That leaves Tasmania – where Labor has walked away from holding power for the last decade – and the Brisbane City Council as the most stable of the nation's Liberal strongholds.

Abbott was at least an ideologue, who, like Howard, had a strong view of what he believed Australia should look like. He continued dragging the party to the right, so it was no surprise that Turnbull, while strong enough to wrest the party room vote away from Abbott, was not prepared to handle Abbott and Joyce's personal projects in the shape of even more fringe right MPs, like Queensland's George Christensen.

Scott Morrison was able to come up through the middle using some of Howard's cunning, but his transactional nature meant he only fostered talent in the party that was of the most benefit to him. Peter Dutton was picked to hold the party together on its march to obscurity. No one asked for Sussan Ley, leaving the Liberals being led by someone with no authority in the party room, the branches, the executive or the base.

The Nationals now care so little about the Coalition that they attempted to divorce the Liberals mere weeks after the last election loss, because the Liberals were making noises about not being led around by the nose by their country cousins. The Nationals cannot govern without the Liberals and vice versa, but this has not been about rationality or sense for at least a decade. Now it's about winning the ideological battle within the party. They'll all lose, but they don't care. Howard taught them how to wage ideological fights, but he kept the secret to winning them to himself.

Unlike 2007, when the warning flashes first started, this isn't a rebuilding stage. It's a terminal decline and the inevitable end point of a man who created a party to reflect his own image of how the world should be. The world, and Australia, moved on. The Liberal Party didn't.

Even as it became obvious that Howard's time had come (despite what some members of the press gallery were writing in their columns at the time), he had such a stranglehold over the party that they still couldn't move him on. Costello, who spent at least three years after the Howard government lost power moaning to anyone who would listen about his leadership what ifs, wrote in his own book of that time: 'Two months before the November poll in 2007, he asked the Cabinet to tell him whether he should go. And it did. But he rejected that advice. He loved the job and all that came with it.'

Advice. Even as the end was nigh and Howard was done in the eye of the public, they still couldn't shift him even though it may have saved some marginal seats. He said no; he wasn't challenged. Howard once said, and was proven right, that the times would suit him. They did. And now the Liberal Party he created no longer suits the times.

12
Welfare and Unemployment

'We have a solemn obligation to help those in our community who are deserving of help. Equally we have a right, as a responsible community, to ask of those who are receiving help, where it is reasonable to do so, that they do something in return for that assistance and something that is commensurate with the help and their own circumstances.'[1]

John Howard at the official launch of Centrelink, 1997

In postwar Australia, the one that Howard grew up in, if you needed a job, you could walk into a Commonwealth Employment Service office and they would find you a job. There has never been a question about the work ethic of Australians, it's just sometimes, life happens.

World War II had also brought with it the need for a stronger social security safety net – the Department of Social Services had been created in 1939 and was fully operative by 1941. The widows' pension was established in 1942 and included deserted wives, divorced women and women whose husbands were in prison or hospital. In 1943, the Commonwealth introduced funeral benefits, a wife allowance was set up for incapacitated or injured men with a spouse, and in 1945, unemployment and sickness benefits in the form of flat rate payments were established. A High Court challenge on the validity of the government using consolidated revenue to finance the payments led to the 1946 Social Services referendum. Australia voted yes and in 1947, the social services act consolidated all the various payments under one piece of legislation. Australia had a social security net.

At first, this was widely accepted as necessary and a social good. By the 1970s, though, the culture wars were well and truly whirring up. From 1946 to 1975, Australia's national unemployment rate sat, on average, below 2 per cent, with both Labor and Coalition governments using deficit spending to maintain full employment (and yes, that mostly meant white and male). But by 1975, neoliberalism was taking hold and stagflation, frustration at industrial disputes (in the 1950s, there had been about 1300 strikes a year on average; by the 1970s, it was 2370) and deregulation moves across the global economy saw Australia abandon full employment for the 'natural' rate of unemployment, which would help keep a lid on inflation (and we still use this today).[2]

But stagflation (slowing growth, rising unemployment, rising inflation) had taken hold, which meant more people were relying on unemployment benefits than had previously been the case, and abandoning full employment as a policy only added to it. It was around that time that the 'dole bludger' myth really started to take hold, and conservative forces began to stir discontent among the working class over people receiving money without having to do the work. If you have ever come across someone complaining that people who receive a fortnightly stipend that falls well under the poverty line are 'living large' on welfare or words to that effect, it is a hangover from this time, where minimum wage and unemployment payments were closer.

But it hasn't been that way for a long time. Australia spent the decades between the shift from full employment to the Howard election demonising the unemployed for political gain. Howard's 1996 election platform contained a promise to address this. Again, Labor had paved the way. The 'tough savings' budget, delivered by Hawke and Keating in 1987 (and continued in the next couple of years), included cuts to community employment programs, the widows' pension, Medicare and unemployment benefits.

In 1993, as prime minister, Keating announced the six-month job guarantee as part of the 'Working Nation' package, which was meant to tackle long-term unemployment. It at least contained recognition that prolonged unemployment was just as much a structural problem as it was a result of economic cycles.

When Howard came along in 1996, he was determined to expand neoliberal policy across Australia, and that meant 'restructuring' our welfare system. Social security language shifted from 'entitlements' for citizens to their 'obligations' for receiving something from the state.[3]

Or, in simpler parlance, the deserving and the undeserving.

In line with Howard's world view, pensioners were deserving. Families were deserving. The middle and upper class was deserving (he was doing all of this at the same time as setting up his spend-a-thon in tax breaks for middle and upper Australia). But those on unemployment benefits? They needed to prove they deserved the help.

It was a project that took years but is now so firmly entrenched that Labor governments have continued the punch down on the unemployed policy.

Howard was elected vowing to cut 'waste' from every government department bar defence, with public servants and the social security budget to face the biggest axes.

The Liberal Party had created their 'ordinary' family that they built many of their policies and lines around attracting during the lead-up to the 1996 campaign using research and polling led by Andrew Robb and Mark Textor. Textor came up with 'Phil and Jenny', two archetypal swing voters, who had been married for eight years. Pamela Williams, in her book *The Victory: The inside story of the takeover of Australia*, describes Phil and Jenny as thirty-eight and thirty-four with a six-year-old son. Phil earns $30,000 as a head warehouseman and Jenny works two part-time jobs cleaning and behind a counter, because she wanted to be home for six-year-old Jason. Their Commodore needs a service. Their mortgage had them stretched and worried about interest rates. They had heard of the economic boom but not experienced it, and they couldn't stand Keating. They paid taxes, but the rich were getting richer and minorities were getting special handouts – and they were getting nothing.

Howard and the Liberals could work with that. Talking to Phil and Jenny gave them their campaign, and Phil and Jenny's anger helped form what became known in political circles as 'welfare antagonism' in the community. Howard responded with a policy that would take $1 billion in cuts from social security over three years and deliver it to families earning $40,000–$70,000. Phil and Jenny would be incentivised for Jenny to stop doing the part-time jobs she hated and stay home and keep house for Phil and Jason, and they would receive tax breaks for being a good little battling family. Maybe they could afford to have that second kid!

And those on welfare? Well, they needed to start meeting their 'mutual obligations' to Australian taxpayers like Phil and Jenny and show some responsibility. 'Welfare to work' was the first buzz phrase and it very quickly became 'work for the dole'. This wasn't about training people, or even preparing them formally for the workforce, it was literally about having people carry out menial labour and tasks for the dollar amount of their unemployment payment. That was no longer a social security benefit or entitlement, because you couldn't consider yourself entitled to welfare without proving you were deserving.

In making that delineation clear, the Department of Social Services would no longer deliver payments, a new agency called Centrelink would do that, in what was set up as a 'purchaser–provider split'. Centrelink was set up to save the government money and monitor the new responsibilities being placed on job seekers.[4]

At the launch of Centrelink in September 1997, Howard said the agency was the realisation of one of his longest held political desires to streamline public agencies:

> The consolidation in Centrelink of so many of the services of the government that interact with people will provide, of course, a more human face. It will provide a more efficient service. It will lead to far less public dissatisfaction. And very importantly, it will give a new sense of career and a new sense of career opportunity to the thousands of people who work for Centrelink. Because Centrelink is carving out a new horizon and a completely different horizon. And it's a demonstration that there is an Australian way, a unique Australian way, of delivering service

> support to those in the community who deserve and need our help and our assistance.[5]

By 2001, the minister overseeing Centrelink, Amanda Vanstone, had to ask for additional call centre funding as calls from 25,000 people a day (or about 85 per cent) could not reach an operator. That has not improved.[6]

It is probably worth mentioning here that Centrelink's job, unlike the Commonwealth Employment Service, was not to get people into work, but to monitor them as they looked for it, by meeting the new 'mutual obligations' Howard set up. A new 'job network' of public and private interests was established to 'help' people find jobs. They would do this by 'competing' to find people work. The abuses open to the scheme were immediately obvious, but that didn't stop the scheme from not only going ahead, it rapidly expanded.

And as for the people who would be relying on Centrelink to provide their payments? Well, if they were unemployed, they had to start proving themselves:

> If we are to realise the true potential of Australia as we move into the twenty-first century, we must constantly look to ways of not only improving the efficiency with which the private sector of our economy operates but also the efficiency and the compassion with which services to the less fortunate, in particular, in our community, operate.

> We need, as far as possible, to take away the notion of dependency from the delivery of services. We need to develop a balance between compassion and responsibility. We need to deliver services in an efficient and friendly manner but, nonetheless, with an eye to our overall obligations to the taxpayers of Australia who pay for the services and the support which is delivered to others within the community.[7]

Over the next eleven years, Howard completely reshaped how we view welfare and made the lives of those needing to access the system so much harder than it needed to be – then and now.

'The election of the Howard government marked a paradigm shift in welfare policy with the implementation of far-reaching reforms around the concept of mutual obligation,' academics Shaun Wilson and Nick Turnbull at the University of New South Wales concluded in a paper looking at Howard's use of 'wedge' politics.[8]

'Howard's new welfare paradigm defined welfare as a problem associated with "dependency culture" and linked reforms to specific social groups (single mothers, young unemployed, new migrants).'

The Howard government defunded welfare advocacy groups, including the Australian Youth Affairs Coalition and National Shelter, and then set about limiting the access and reach of interest groups like the Australian Council of Social Service (ACOSS), which received some government funding. In August 1999, the government sent out a 'request' that funded bodies work 'collaboratively with the Department of Family and Community Services and provide early warning for all controversial issues planned for media coverage that might attract public comment.' This was seen as muzzling criticism, but if that wasn't clear enough, the Howard government released the draft Charities Bill that threatened to remove tax exemptions and concessions from organisations 'whose purpose was deemed to be "attempting to change the law or government policy" if such action were "more than ancillary or incidental to their core purpose"'.[9]

That particular law didn't get put through, but the threat remained (and has no matter who has been leading the Coalition since). In his 2008 paper, 'Retrenching or renovating the Australian welfare state: The paradox of the Howard government's neo-liberalism', academic Philip Mendes also notes the Howard government had the Institute of Public Affairs audit non-government groups like ACOSS, and threatened to establish its own peak interest group for social service to undermine ACOSS's position.

Instead of radically changing who was able to apply for welfare, Howard carried out his death by a thousand cuts approach and slowly kept making changes to eligibility criteria, so only those having to deal with the system knew the extent of just how hard it was. Labor's activity test (how many hours someone must spend looking for work) for unemployment was tightened, penalties for non-compliance with the rules increased, rent assistance for single people living in share accommodation was reduced, youth allowances were means-tested, a two-year waiting period was installed for new immigrants, and liquid asset waiting periods were set for anyone wanting to apply, meaning someone had to drain their savings before they were able to access a payment.

In 1999, it became all about 'welfare dependency', and figures released by the government spoke of a jump in people receiving unemployment payments long term, claiming a jump from 10 per cent in 1978 to 18 per cent in 1998, or about 2.6 million people. Mendes's research showed the government relied on 'statistical illusion, reflecting a large shift from full-time work to casual and part-time work, increased divorce rates, the introduction of supplementary payments to low-income working families and other changes to eligibility criteria'.

There had been a lot of hype around 'welfare dependency', and in 1996, three young Australian siblings became the punching bag of the nation when *A Current Affair* painted them as 'dole bludging' teenagers who refused to work. The teens, the eldest of whom was eighteen at the time, were pilloried for their hair and their attitude, for living at home and sleeping in. The show set them up in jobs thousands of kilometres from their home and then acted shocked when the teens quit.

The Howard government used the anger to build permission to go even harder. Work for the Dole was trialled in 1997 and became policy in 1998. All unemployed people aged between eighteen and twenty-four who had received payments for six months or more were made to join the scheme. The following year, it was expanded to include all school leavers who left before completing Year 12 if they didn't find a job in three months. *The Courier-Mail* reported that Tony Abbott – then the minister for employment services – had delivered a speech where he said:

> To leave people on welfare is cruelty. It's cruelty masquerading as compassion. What has happened far too much over the last two decades is that people have gone on welfare and disappeared into the system, only to emerge years later as part of the problem of intergenerational welfare dependency.[10]

Work for the Dole was scaled up.

Unemployed people in Sydney became an unpaid workforce for the 2000 Summer Olympic Games. By December 2000, the upper age limit was increased to thirty-nine and others were encouraged to volunteer. In 2002, to appease the Nationals, private agricultural properties experiencing drought became eligible to receive Work for the Dole participants. (Free labour for farmers – where have we seen those policies before?)

Then–Minister for Employment Services, Mal Brough, circulated segments of what turned out to be a highly controversial report, which claimed 16 per cent of job seekers were 'cruisers' – i.e. people who were 'happy' to be unemployed and did not want to find work.

'If these so-called cruisers think the Howard government is going to allow them to take advantage of the generosity of the Australian taxpayer to fund their lifestyle choice, they have another thing coming,' Brough said at the time. 'If this particular group of people feel relaxed about being unemployed, I intend to make them feel a lot less comfortable and far more active.'[11] (In 2015, Tony Abbott would later refuse to apologise for saying taxpayers shouldn't have to bear the burden of paying for the 'lifestyle choice' of Indigenous people living in remote communities.)

It was a nice little call back to Howard's 'comfortable and relaxed' cohort and making it clear that the unemployed did not deserve such luxuries. Us and them, in a new way.

By the Rudd election, people had to work for fifty hours throughout the fortnight across approved community or social groups, or the Army reserve (and whatever other private interest group expressed an interest in free labour). Rudd didn't drop it. Neither did Julia Gillard (although under her government quiet changes were made). It was all for nothing – when Abbott won he made it even bigger. After the death of eighteen-year-old Josh Park-Fing while on a Work for the Dole placement, and growing reports of unsafe work conditions, injuries and concerns of exploitation, the Youth Jobs PaTH program was set up as an alternative internship program for people under twenty-five. Businesses would be paid to take on the interns. Work for the Dole still exists and it's still just as hopeless at helping people into work.

The Howard government also waged war on people who were on the Disability Support Pension (DSP) and single parents, and in 2005, the government made it much, much harder to receive the DSP. Thousands of people were pushed into the mutual obligations system for the unemployed, and the mercy of job providers, despite their limited work capacity.

That became even harder the following year, when the Howard government halved how much additional paid work someone on the DSP could do before their pension was impacted, to fifteen hours a week.

As all of this was happening, tax breaks and subsidies were being handed over to middle class families, as Howard cemented his 'battlers' base. In 2013, the International Monetary Fund (IMF) reviewed 200 years of government records and found two periods of 'fiscal profligacy' in Australia, both occurring under Howard – the start of the mining boom in 2003 and his final years in office between 2005–07.[12] In 2004, the government announced a one-off payment for every baby born, starting at $3000, and increased on a staggered schedule to $5000 per baby. It cost billions, and research by e61 Institute into the scheme released in late 2025 found it did contribute to more babies (estimating an additional 16,250 children born in the first year).[13]

The mutual obligations system has been judged a billion-dollar failure, which not only punishes people on unemployment benefits, it actively makes it harder for them to find suitable work. A 2023 Labor government inquiry into the system reported:

> Social Ventures Australia (SVA) and the Antipoverty Centre highlighted a study of impacts of mutual obligation on 6000 unemployed people using the Household, Income and Labour Dynamics in Australia (HILDA) Survey data. The HILDA data showed jobseekers who were subject to mutual obligation took longer to find employment than those who were not. The study also found that when mutual obligations did help jobseekers find work, the jobs were typically lower paid or lower skilled.[14]

Despite a 650-page report finding all the ways the system had failed people and was costing taxpayers money, the Albanese government concluded it had become so big, it would be too difficult to scrap.[15] The system will cost $9.5 billion between 2024 and 2028, which makes it the largest single government procurement outside of defence, but for very little gain (both for the public and jobseekers). But Howard's dream was so successful, there is no longer the capability within the public service to pull it back from private job providers.

In late 2025, the Albanese government was facing what unemployment and poverty advocates were calling 'Robodebt 2.0' after it was discovered that private job providers were unlawfully cancelling or suspending people's unemployment payments for real or imagined failures to meet 'mutual obligations' under the system. It had been cancelling or suspending various parts of the system to try and head off another national scandal, but even Robodebt itself, which is now considered a national shame, took way too long to reach the public consciousness, much because Australia has been taught not to care about the unemployed.

The attitude since the Howard years is that being unemployed is an individual moral failing and those who fail must pay society back for the taxpayer help, when in actuality the enforcement of mutual obligation policies and the demonisation of an entire cohort of people is a sign of societal moral decline. Howard was happy to give tax breaks to people who didn't need it, to pay landowners to take care of their land, to pay businesses to hire Australians and placed no obligations on any of them in return.

Howard and the Coalition have so successfully demonised people for not working, we accept the punishments meted out to them by the government through job providers and mutual obligations as necessary. While it is clear from the data that the rate of the unemployment payment and other associated payments are keeping people in poverty and are a barrier to finding suitable work, permanently raising the rate above the poverty line is considered 'political suicide'. Our government policy is to keep people unemployed to help lower inflation, but then we punish the people who are taking one for Team Australia. As Howard was introducing his system of mutual obligations and telling Australians who was deserving of help and who wasn't, he was slashing the social schemes that helped people stay afloat, undermining the industrial relations system to make work less secure, giving employers more power, getting rid of unfair dismissal laws, making university and vocational training more expensive, increasing the cost of housing, and dividing Australians over race, class and their education status.

Phil and Jenny, the imaginary couple the Howard campaign built their policies around in 1996, probably benefitted, but god forbid what would have happened to them if they divorced, or Phil was laid off.

By that time, though, all the other Phils and Jennys wouldn't have had much sympathy for them. Such is the Howard legacy – compassion, empathy and assistance are contingent on whether someone else thinks you deserve it, with the people enforcing the judgements usually the ones the safety net was originally built to catch. That was one of Howard's greatest tricks.

Conclusion

> 'When I look back I think that most of the things I wanted to do, I got done.'[1]
>
> John Howard, 2018

There is so much more that could be written. How Howard changed the public broadcaster and helped set it up for decades of cowed leadership. How he aped sporting heroes, borrowing the sheen of our national teams, but then convinced Australians that sports and politics didn't mix. How he changed views on marriage, divorce and a woman's place. How he survived what should have been politically unsustainable. The national security apparatus that is almost impossible to ignore. The nobbling of the public service, the lowering of ministerial standards. The trashing of our institutions. The condemnation of the arts. The personal infringements in the name of 'national security'. It's almost impossible to examine any part of modern Australian society and not come across Howard's palm print as he shoved it in another direction.

There is an apocryphal story of how Margaret Thatcher was asked what she considered her greatest achievement, and she supposedly answered, 'Tony Blair'.

You could say John Howard's greatest achievement is the modern Labor Party. Even with the historical majority it won in 2025, and the complete cratering of the Liberal Party vote, Labor seems afraid of making any sort of progressive change because of what *could* happen, of how someone could twist the debate and send them back into the political wilderness. Even with another term guaranteed following the next election (that is just maths – the Coalition just cannot get there and are also showing no signs of even wanting to try), Labor is tiptoeing around the need for reform, still haunted by the ghost of Howard's Australia. Howard sucked up the political air so comprehensively, he's still taking it from the lungs of those who would stand against him. The Liberal Party might be done and dusted, but Howard's politics have spooked the Labor Party into taking its place in the political ecosystem.

Howard's legacy has been to rob Australian politics of any sort of progressive bravery and to replace it with 'governance', as if slow and steady can fend off despair. It can't. It just pulls us all further to the right. And yet it is never enough. Australians now just accept that it's normal to make people on welfare earn their meagre subsistence, that you don't deserve to live even at the poverty line if you're not producing measurable labour now. They accept that people seeking asylum deserve to be locked up offshore, with less rights than animals. That to criticise the flag or Australia's colonial history is to be anti-Australian and deserving of public stoning. That standing with America, no matter what it does, is the Australian way. That Indigenous people are to live as second-class citizens in their own country. That calling someone racist is worse than being racist. That looking after the rich was 'aspiration' in action.

Howard made lying in politics an art form, and was so good at it that it is now completely normalised. His 'never ever' on GST was only ever a 'not now'. Core and non-core promises are part of the political lexicon, allowing conservative governments to say what they wish and then just wait until they can get away with it to do what they want. Public backlash never stopped Howard; it emboldened him. If the Port Arthur massacre happened in Howard's second term and not a couple of months into his job as prime minister, it is doubtful that we would have the gun laws even Howard's most strident critics have had to give him credit for. Because while Howard liked to say that the public knew who he was – 'I often used to joke that I encountered a lot of people who would say I can't stand you, but I know what you stand for' – the truth is, we didn't.

Howard was a political chameleon, guided by his own cobbled together ideologies, grievances and identity beliefs, and when it was clear he didn't really fit in where he was, he just changed where he was to fit him.

Looking up Howard's various regrets since leaving office, there are no apologies for any of the lies, the racism, the inequality, the divisions, the policy missteps, the embracement of the far right, the harm, the fights, or the consequences.

He has listed, at various times, the shocking right-arm pies he bowled the Pakistani army while visiting Pakistan in 2005; wearing a bulletproof vest when he spoke to farmers about the gun laws; taking too long to respond to the Wik High Court decision (but not how he responded); and not getting rid of the no-disadvantage test in WorkChoices.

He was honest in what he told journalist David Speers in Vietnam all those years ago – 'And if I ever develop reservations, well, I hope I would have the grace to keep them to myself' – because if he does have any reservations about the Australia he created, we don't hear about it.

'When I look back I think that most of the things I wanted to do, I got done,' he told a relaxed and comfortable group of students in Oxford in 2012.[2]

The myth that Howard was (overwhelmingly) popular during his eleven years as prime minister is largely aimed at keeping his legacy intact. The truth is that his government lost the popular vote in 1998, and the Coalition's primary vote wasn't too different from the decade before. The opinion polls were often in Labor's favour – but the party had been so successfully wedged by Howard time and time again, that they kept self-sabotaging in who they elected as leader to face him. Howard knew he didn't have to win the country – just enough of those soft, undecided voters somewhat uncertain with Labor's offering that they reluctantly stuck with what they knew.

He was so successful at it, he confounded Labor for eleven years and prompted Kevin Rudd to campaign as a conservative, cautious Labor leader. Howard was so good at what he did, he had his opponents turning themselves inside out to appeal to him. Howard shifted the working class from Labor to the Liberal Party and exploited their aspiration for more for his own gain. Little Capitalists became little investors, screwing over everyone who was to come up after them. Author and commentator Tim Dunlop sums up Howard's success succinctly:

> A key plank of John Howard's modus operandi was to use such cultural appeals, particularly to men, to reset the idea of the working class from being an alignment whose material interests could be served by the collective action of unions, labour protections and wage stability to one in which they were recast as individuals – rugged individuals, no less – competing in a deregulated economy.[3]

Howard would just say he was speaking for 'ordinary Australians'.

Because, say what you want about Howard, the man knew how to use power. He still does, timing his interventions for maximum impact. Howard has not gone quietly into the night, but when he speaks (which is often) it is not greeted with the usual 'former prime ministers should be seen and not heard', it's lionised as if words have come down from the mount.

Which, in a way, they have. When Howard speaks there is still a good chunk of Australians who listen, and many of them sit in the parliament. Howard used power so comprehensively, he has all but robbed modern Labor of being able to do the same. Howard did not care about bipartisanship. He didn't for a moment think he couldn't change the country because the Labor opposition were not on board. He just did it.

He also didn't care about being criticised, seeing it as proof he was doing the right thing; after all, people had criticised Thatcher, and Howard believed she had not only *not* done anything wrong, but had saved the United Kingdom. Howard didn't need a bullhorn, he allowed people to read into the gaps in between what he was saying, or not saying. Howard's silences, what he chose not to defend, or condemn, often did the talking for him. Howard would suggest something in one breath and take it away with the other.

Take how he explained not apologising to Indigenous Australians, for example:

> I've explained why, I don't believe the current generation can be held accountable for the injustices inflicted by earlier generations, particularly when those practices were sanctioned by law at the time. I am personally very sorry; I think we all are for any injustice. But it's not a lack of sympathy or empathy or sensitivity, it's just a belief of mine and I hold it very sincerely. It's not based on an opinion poll, it's just a genuine belief that I hold and it's not just myself but the whole government holds that view.[4]

He's sorry but he's not sorry, he's not apologising and it's not based on opinion polls, or the public mood, or anything other than his own core beliefs, which were very personal and sincere, and coincidentally, the views of the entire government.

The great Mungo MacCallum once somewhat cheekily defined a politician as 'a man or woman who honestly and sincerely believes that the worst thing that could happen to the country is for him or her to be voted out of office'.[5] Howard truly believed the greatest ill that could befall the country was for him to lose an election.

And when it happened and he not only lost government, but his electorate, Howard just changed how he used his power, channelling it through protégés like Abbott, Morrison and Dutton. He is still trotted out on the election hustings, still placed on the front page of the newspapers and still holding court with those who would have power, because he always truly believed that if you want to change the country, you change the country. And you don't need permission to do it.

There was not a moment where Howard thought he needed to ask permission for the intervention, or to take Australia to war, or to turn the nation's back on its legal and moral obligations to accept asylum seekers. Howard didn't ask permission to change the nation's gun laws, or the tax system, or to privatise national services. He didn't think to check with the unions or the Labor Party about IR or WorkChoices. He didn't spend years building a social licence to realign Australia with the United States, or to destroy the republic, or give tax handouts to the rich.

He. Just. Did. It.

And sure, there were losses. And moments where he took it all too far and had to backtrack. But he never backed down on what he truly believed needed to happen. WorkChoices may have cost him the final election and his seat of Bennelong, but Howard would probably tell you it was worth it – because much of it continues to this day. Howard wasn't booted from politics wondering about 'what ifs'. The man did what he set out to do – change the nation. It's just too bad we don't seem to have anyone willing to ape his bravery and follow suit, but with reforms that would better reflect what it actually means to be Australian, and deliver what the country needs now, rather than remain trapped by what seems possible under the rules set by one man, three decades ago.

Our lives are still being impacted by that man's arrested development and yet we are rapidly reaching the point in time where people will have no idea who he is.

The year before his election, Howard told the ABC: 'We want to assert the very principle that truth is absolute, truth is supreme, truth is never disposable in national political life.'

And so, let us finally, thirty years later, tell the truth on Howard: He gutted the nation's soul.

Howard made us crueller and suspicious of others, jealous for what we didn't have and angry at those who had less.

Australia may have been in a once-in-a-generation economic boom, but we fell into a culture recession and moral deficit under his government.

We must also bear responsibility. We have perpetuated his worst instincts and sat numbly as successive governments did the same.

It doesn't mean there is no hope for change. If there is anything to learn from Howard, it is how to use power to do what you think is best and not seek permission to do so. Howard may have screwed us, but it is the governments, particularly those from Labor, who have come after and kept his version of the nation, unwilling to push back against his legacy while bearing the brunt of its consequences, who let him do it.

Howard may have diminished us, but his successors are the ones who have kept us down.

Three decades on, we may finally have reached the point of no more. Howard has spent those decades continuing to wage his war against who Australia might have been and what we might have become without him, spurred by the belief that the battle of ideas is never completely won.

He's right about that of course, but not much else. Howard's political legacy has largely been the battle of those ideas, and how he constantly shifted the goal posts and won by having both sides play by his rules.

But the times no longer suit him, or us. And we are not relaxed and comfortable. That's not a bad thing – you can't win the future by being relaxed and comfortable in the past. It's not just science that progresses one funeral at a time; it can be countries as well. Howard might have owned our immediate past, but he is irrelevant in our future. Our next battle? Convincing those who have the power to make the necessary changes to believe it.

Notes

Introduction

1 **Self-reliance, a fair go, pulling together, and having a go . . .** From a speech by Prime Minister John Howard to the Melbourne Press Club, 22 November 2000. Accessed via: <australianpolitics.com/2000/11/22/john-howard-distinct-enduring-australian-values.html/>.

2 **Living proof of the Orwellian dictum . . .** From a speech by the Leader of the Opposition, John Howard, on National Identity, one of a series given during 1995, 13 December 1995. Accessed via: <australianpolitics.com/1995/12/13/national-identity-howard-headland-speech.html/>.

Chapter 1: Culture Wars

1 **I think in public life you take a position . . .** From a speech by Prime Minister John Howard at the Australian Chamber of Commerce, Sheraton on the Park, Sydney, 2 October 2002. Accessed via: <pmtranscripts.pmc.gov.au/release/transcript-12931>.

2 **Anne Summers's reflection on how Howard shaped the times . . .** From Anne Summers, 'The sad times do suit him; he made them', *Sydney Morning Herald*, 18 August 2003, <smh.com.au/national/the-sad-times-do-suit-him-he-made-them-20030818-gdh9fe.html>.

3 **You shouldn't get so hung up, you shouldn't be so politically correct . . .** Quote from John Howard in a 1996 *Four Corners* interview with Liz Jackson. As quoted in 'John Howard is a not so secret Bob Dylan fan', Crikey, 14 October 2016, <crikey.com.au/2016/10/14/john-howard-not-secret-bob-dylan-fan/>.

4 **It was we who did the dispossessing . . .** From a speech by Prime Minister Paul Keating at the Australian Launch of the International Year for the World's Indigenous People, Redfern, 10 December 1992. Accessed via: pmtranscripts.pmc.gov.au/sites/default/files/original/00008765.pdf

5 **An average Australian bloke . . .** Quote from John Howard in a *Four Corners* interview in 1996, From Barbara McMahon, 'A Lazarus from Down Under', *Guardian Australia*, 12 November 2007, <theguardian.com/world/2007/nov/11/australia.barbaramcmahon>.

6 **No society which has a proper understanding of its history . . .** From a speech by Prime Minister John Howard in an address to Australia Day Council's Australia Day Luncheon, Darling Harbour, Sydney, 24 January 1997. Accessed via: <pmtranscripts.pmc.gov.au/release/transcript-10217>.

7 **In facing the realities of the past . . .** From a speech by Prime Minister John Howard in an opening address to the Australian Reconciliation Convention, Melbourne, 26 May 1997. Accessed via: <pmtranscripts.pmc.gov.au/release/transcript-10361>.

8 **This 'black armband' view of our past . . .** From a speech by Prime Minister John Howard in an address at the Sir Robert Menzies Lecture, The Liberal Tradition, the Beliefs and Values Which Guide the Federal Government, 19 November 1996. Accessed via: <pmtranscripts.pmc.gov.au/release/transcript-10171>.

9 **Today we join the past with the present . . .** From a speech by Prime Minister John Howard at the Launch of the Gallipoli 2000 Campaign, 11 April 2000. Accessed via: <pmtranscripts.pmc.gov.au/release/transcript-22698>.

10 **Australians are free to be proud of their country . . .** From Prime Minister John Howard's draft Australian Constitutional Preamble, 1999. Accessed via: <abc.net.au/ra/federasi/tema2/preamble_eng.htm>.

11 **I didn't want to give it up . . .** Prime Minister John Howard in an interview with Kerry O'Brien for the *7.30 Report*, ABC, 11 August 1999. Accessed via: <pmtranscripts.pmc.gov.au/release/transcript-10998>.

12 **Anzac is a myth of White Australia . . .** Quote from Martin Ball in 'What the Anzac Revival means', *The Age*, 24 April 2004, <theage.com.au/national/what-the-anzac-revival-means-20040424-gdxq7h.html>.

13 **Howard said that he didn't think it was wrong, racist, immoral or anything else . . .** A quote from John Howard in 1988 to *The Age*, 'Howard reasserts right to decide cultural identity', 20 September 1988, quoted in Michael Carey, 'Australia Day remains a culture war battleground: "If Australia Day falls the left will be out of control"', NITV, 23 January 2018, <sbs.com.au/nitv/article/opinion-australia-day-remains-a-culture-war-battleground-if-australia-day-falls-the-left-will-be-out-of-control/6rnr189rw>.

14 **I do hold the view that the luckiest thing that happened to this country was . . .** Quote from John Howard in an interview with *The Australian*, July 2023. As quoted in Hannah Ritchie, 'Colonisation by the British "luckiest thing" to happen to Australia – John Howard', BBC News, 26 July 2023, <bbc.com/news/world-australia-66309637>.

15 **It would, however, be a crushing mistake to downplay the hopes and expectations . . .** Prime Minister John Howard in an address to the National Press Club, Great Hall, Parliament House, 25 January 2006. Accessed via: <pmtranscripts.pmc.gov.au/release/transcript-22110>.

16 **The subsequent report was kept secret, until [. . .] its eventual release . . .** by Andrew Jakubowicz, 'Racism, anti-racism campaigns and Australian social research: a case study in recovering socially-useful knowledge', <andrewjakubowicz.com/publications/antiracism1998>.

17 **There was no need to reconstruct Australian identity . . .** From Carol Johnson's book *Governing Change: Keating to Howard*, 2000, University of Queensland Press.

18 **We put it in there because . . .** John Howard speaking to NewsCorp about the moves he made to stop marriage equality from progressing. As quoted in 'John Howard stands by his government's bans on same-sex marriage', OUTinPerth, 1 January 2025, < outinperth.com/john-howard-stands-by-his-governments-bans-on-same-sex-marriage/>.

19 **I'm against gay adoption . . .** Prime Minister John Howard speaking on John Laws's radio program. As quoted in 'Howard slams ACT gay adoption law', *Sydney Morning Herald*, 8 March 2004.

Chapter 2: Housing

1 **Anybody who owns a house is very happy . . .** Prime Minister John Howard in an interview with Steve Austin, ABC Radio Brisbane,

19 September 2003. Accessed via: <pmtranscripts.pmc.gov.au/release/transcript-20920>.

2 **Investor housing accounted for 30 per cent of the stock of housing loans . . .** From the International Monetary Fund report, *Australia: Staff Report for the 2003 Article IV Consultation*, September 3, 2003. Accessed via: <imf.org/external/pubs/ft/scr/2003/cr03336.pdf>.

3 Interview with Steve Austin.

4 **His intent to 'aid' 'little Capitalists' . . .** From a speech by Opposition Leader Robert Menzies, Museum of Australian Democracy at Old Parliament House, Melbourne, 10 November 1949. Accessed via: <electionspeeches.moadoph.gov.au/speeches/1949-robert-menzies>.

5 **Little Capitalists . . .** A comment by the Labor Minister for Postwar Reconstruction, John Dedman, in a parliamentary housing debate on 2 October 1945. Quoted in 'Sir Robert Menzies's little capitalists', Robert Menzies Institute, <robertmenziesinstitute.org.au/research-project/home-ownership-and-menzies-government/>.

6 **Data obtained by the ABC from the Australian Taxation Office . . .** A statistic from ATO data obtained by the ABC quoted in Geraden Cann, 'Landlords, property investors, Australia renters market housing', ABC News, 17 October 2024, <abc.net.au/news/2024-10-17/landlords-property-investors-australia-renters-market-housing/104421798>.

7 **In 1999, the median house price in Sydney . . .** A statistic from Peter Abelson and Demi Chung, 'The Real Story of Housing Prices in Australia from 1970 to 2003', Applied Economics, 2006, <appliedeconomics.com.au/wp-content/uploads/2021/10/2006-real-story-of-house-prices-australia-1970-2003.pdf>.

8 **In 2025, it was 1.7 million . . .** A statistic from Nerida Conisbee, 'New data shows dramatic change in Aussie house prices, realestate.com.au, 30 September 2025, <realestate.com.au/news/new-data-shows-dramatic-change-in-aussie-house-prices/>.

9 **The richest 10 per cent of Australians receive . . .** A statistic from Greg Jericho, 'The awful truth at the heart of Australian housing policy', *The Guardian*, 15 February 2024, <theguardian.com/business/grogonomics/2024/feb/15/the-awful-truth-at-the-heart-of-australian-housing-policy>.

10 **The PC had noted negative gearing and the CGT concession had . . .** A quote from the Productivity Commission quoted in Shane Wright, 'House prices were already spiralling in 2004: Here's what Howard and Costello did about it', *Sydney Morning Herald*, 1 January 2025.

11 **Unlike those parents, who took on loans . . .** A statistic from Leonie Thorne, 'Generation "screwed": How gen Z and millennial housing concerns are shaping the election', ABC News, 19 April 2025, <abc.net.au/news/2025-04-19/election-targets-gen-z-millennial-renting-housing-property-woes/105184534>.

Chapter 3: Race

1 **I do not accept that there is underlying racism in this country . . .** From a speech by Prime Minister John Howard on the Cronulla race riots at a press conference, Phillip Street, Sydney, 12 December 2005. Accessed via: <pmtranscripts.pmc.gov.au/release/transcript-22077>.

2 Ibid.

3 **There are family suspicions he was a member of the New Guard . . .** A quote by Milton Cockburn on his profile of Lyall Howard for the *Herald*, 7 January 1989, quoted in Alan Ramsey, 'By the people, for the powerful', *Sydney Morning Herald*, 26 November 2005, <smh.com.au/national/by-the-people-for-the-powerful-20051126-gdmiqk.html>.

4 **The New Guard membership application form . . .** As quoted on the National Archives of Australia website, 'The New Guard'. Accessed via: <naa.gov.au/explore-collection/intelligence-and-security/history-australian-intelligence-and-security/new-guard>.

5 **[Our] family had a real us-and-them thing . . .** A quote from Marion Maddox's book, *God Under Howard: The rise of the religious right in Australian politics*, 2005, Allen & Unwin.

6 **The cherished symbols of Howard's world reveal a process . . .** A quote from Fiona Allon's book, *Renovation Nation: Our Obsession with Home*, 2009, New South/UNSW Press.

7 **If we are ever going to achieve a situation in which . . .** From a speech from John Howard during Hansard – House of Representatives, 5 March 1975. Accessed via: <parlinfo.aph.gov.au/parlInfo/search/display/display.w3p;query=Id%3A%22hansard80%2Fhansardr80%2F1975-03-05%2F0151%22>.

8 **The objection I have to multiculturalism is . . .** John Howard in an interview with Gerard Henderson, January 1989, quoted in Edmund Rice Centre submission to the Senate Select Committee on Strengthening Multiculturalism, 12 May 2017. Accessed via: <aph.gov.au/DocumentStore.ashx?id=70175211-eb7c-4edc-bfef-cd930c103b60&subId=511199>.

9 **One of the great changes that have come over Australia in the last six months . . .** From a speech by Prime Minister John Howard in an address to the Queensland Division of the Liberal Party State Council, 22 September 1996. Accessed via: <pmtranscripts.pmc.gov.au/release/transcript-10114>.

10 **Howard was forced to condemn . . .** Prime Minister John Howard quoted in 'Howard condemns Ku Klux Klan photo', *The Age*, 12 November 2004, <theage.com.au/national/howard-condemns-ku-klux-klan-photo-20041112-gdyz95.html>.

11 **On the Cronulla race riots . . .** From National Museum of Australia, 'Cronulla race riots', National Museum of Australia website, <nma.gov.au/defining-moments/resources/cronulla-race-riots>.

12 **I have always taken a more optimistic view of the character of the Australian people . . .** From a speech by Prime Minister John Howard on the Cronulla race riots at a press conference, Phillip Street, Sydney, 12 December 2005. Accessed via: <pmtranscripts.pmc.gov.au/release/transcript-22077>.

13 Ibid.

14 **I've said generally of migrants who come to this country . . .** Comments made by Prime Minister John Howard on talkback radio, 1 September 2006, quoted in Conor Duffy, 'PM stands by Muslim integration comments', ABC News, 1 September 2006, <abc.net.au/news/2006-09-01/pm-stands-by-muslim-integration-comments/1253202>.

15 **On Howard's integration plan . . .** 'New plan no problem for "fair dinkum" migrants: Howard', ABC News, 15 September 2006, <abc.net.au/news/2006-09-15/new-plan-no-problem-for-fair-dinkum-migrants-howard/1264478>.

16 Ibid.

17 **Statistics released by the Labor government about the citizenship test . . .** Quoted in Phillip Coorey, 'Bradman out for a duck in citizenship test', *Sydney Morning Herald*, 29 January 2008, <smh.com.

au/national/bradman-out-for-duck-in-citizenship-test-20080129-gdryra.html>.

18 See **On Howard's integration plan . . .**

19 **Peter Dutton on believing Fraser made a mistake with allowing Lebanese settlement in Australia . . .** Peter Dutton quoted in Stephanie Anderson, 'Peter Dutton: Fraser made mistake resettling Lebanese refugees', ABC News, 21 November 2016, <abc.net.au/news/2016-11-21/peter-dutton-fraser-made-mistake-resettling-lebanese-refugees/8043624>.

20 **Well, I suppose I can just hope that people understand . . .** Comments made by Prime Minister John Howard about claims of racism in an interview with Ray Martin on *Ray Martin Presents Up Close and Personal*, 15 August 1998. Accessed via: <pmtranscripts.pmc.gov.au/release/transcript-10666>.

Chapter 4: Indigenous Rights

1 **The debate over Australian history . . .** From a speech by Prime Minister John Howard in an address at the Sir Robert Menzies Lecture, The Liberal Tradition, the Beliefs and Values Which Guide the Federal Government, 19 November 1996. Accessed via: <pmtranscripts.pmc.gov.au/release/transcript-10171>.

2 **In facing the realities of the past . . .** From a speech by Prime Minister John Howard in an opening address to the Australian Reconciliation Convention, Melbourne, 26 May 1997. Accessed via: <pmtranscripts.pmc.gov.au/release/transcript-10361>.

3 **Howard regarding native title claims . . .** Prime Minister John Howard in an interview with Kerry O'Brien for the *7.30 Report*, ABC, 4 September 1997. Accessed via: <pmtranscripts.pmc.gov.au/release/transcript-10469>.

4 **Howard on whether native title claims would apply to suburban backyards . . .** Prime Minister John Howard in an interview with Kerry O'Brien for the *7.30 Report*, ABC, 1 December 1997. Accessed via: <pmtranscripts.pmc.gov.au/release/transcript-10554>.

5 **The decision has just about ended Aboriginal reconciliation . . .** Donald McGauchie on native title claims in 2004, quoted in ANTAR, The Wik Decision Factsheet, <antar.org.au/wp-content/uploads/2022/10/Wik-Decision-Factsheet.pdf>.

6 **That funding cut led to a 30 per cent reduction in programs . . .** Statistics in Alison Holland, 'Many claim Australia's longest-running Indigenous body failed – here's why that's wrong', The Conversation, 24 July 2023, <theconversation.com/many-claim-australias-longest-running-indigenous-body-failed-heres-why-thats-wrong-209511>.

7 **The suite was not designed for him . . .** Statement by the architect of Parliament House, John Smith Murdoch. Accessed via: <aph.gov.au/DocumentStore.ashx?id=6d258691-9833-4e34-a973-0a61a2546820>.

8 **Menzies's desk was for a much taller man . . .** From Tony Wright, 'Suite revenge on Chesterfield', *The Age*, 5 December 2007, <theage.com.au/national/suite-revenge-on-chesterfield-20071205-ge6gd3.html>.

9 **Indigenous leaders have repeatedly been told by me . . .** Statement from Prime Minister John Howard on his Amended Wik 10 Point Plan, 8 May 1997, Accessed via: <pmtranscripts.pmc.gov.au/release/transcript-10333>.

10 **Adani using native title 'issues' to lobby Turnbull government . . .** From Natalie Cromb, 'How did the Wik 10-point plan outline our future?', SBS NITV, 8 May 2017 (updated 5 July 2018), <sbs.com.au/nitv/article/how-did-the-wik-10-point-plan-outline-our-future/0i6n8y6uo>.

11 **Turnbull further amended native title legislation . . .** From Paul Gregoire, 'Turnbull clears the way for Indian company to build Adani mine', Sydney Criminal Lawyers Blog, (updated on 25 April 2020), <sydneycriminallawyers.com.au/blog/turnbull-clears-the-way-for-indian-company-to-build-adani-mine>.

12 **I speak for the entire government on this . . .** Prime Minister John Howard on the *7.30 Report* in 2000, quoted in Nakari Thorpe, '7 legacies of John Howard's government', SBS NITV, 3 March 2016 <sbs.com.au/nitv/the-point/article/7-legacies-of-john-howards-government/qj915w31j.

13 **I do not believe that one generation can accept responsibility for the acts of an earlier generation . . .** John Howard speaking with students at the Kennedy School of Government at Harvard, 11 March 2008, quoted in Anne Davies, 'Nothing to say sorry for: Howard', 12 March 2008, *Sydney Morning Herald*, <smh.com.au/national/nothing-to-say-sorry-for-howard-20080312-gds4t6.html>.

Chapter 5: Asylum Seekers and Migration

1 **We will decide who comes to this country . . .** From a speech by Prime Minister John Howard in an address at the launch of 'A Stronger Tasmania Policy', 2 November 2001. Accessed via: <pmtranscripts.pmc.gov.au/release/transcript-12332>.

2 **Howard expected migrants to . . .** From Rick Kuhn, 'Political Review', *The Australian Quarterly*, Vol.61, 1989, p.111. Accessed via: <ppesydney.net/content/uploads/2020/05/Profitability-and-economic-crisis.pdf>.

3 **He wanted migration from Asia to be 'slowed down a little' . . .** From a speech by John Howard in 1988, quoted in Jim Middleton, 'On asylum seekers, our history keeps repeating itself', The Conversation, 14 June 2016, <theconversation.com/on-asylum-seekers-our-history-keeps-repeating-itself-59473>.

4 **Geoffrey Blainey stating that Asia migration should be slowed . . .** Blainey quoted in Paul Kelly's book *The End of Certainty: Power, Politics and Business in Australia*, 1994, Allen & Unwin.

5 **Draw a line on what is increasingly becoming an uncontrollable number of illegal arrivals . . .** Prime Minister John Howard in a radio interview with Neil Mitchell, 3AW, 31 August 2001. Accessed via: <pmtranscripts.pmc.gov.au/release/transcript-12043>.

6 **I should have the right to have a say in who comes into my country . . .** From Pauline Hanson's maiden speech to Parliament, 10 September 1996. Accessed via: <smh.com.au/politics/federal/pauline-hansons-1996-maiden-speech-to-parliament-full-transcript-20160915-grgjv3.html>.

7 See **We will decide who comes to this country . . .**

8 **They irresponsibly sank the damn boat . . .** Prime Minister John Howard speaking on the tenth anniversary of his government in 2006, quoted in Frank Robson, 'Frank Robson reflections on the greatest Australian scandals of the past 30 years', *Sydney Morning Herald*, 27 September 2014, <smh.com.au/lifestyle/frank-robson-reflections-on-the-greatest-australian-scandals-of-the-past-30-years-20140925-10dopd.html>.

9 **If I had been told definitively . . .** John Howard in an interview quoted in Nick Cater's book *The Howard Factor: A Decade that Changed the Nation*, 2006, Melbourne University Publishing.

10 Ibid.

11 **Migration numbers in 2007 were almost double . . .** Statistics available from Australian Bureau of Statistics website. Accessed via: <abs.gov.au/statistics/people/population/national-state-and-territory-population/latest-release>.

12 **Humanitarian visas dropped . . .** Statistics available from Data.gov.au Historical Migration Statistics, created 2 April 2019 (updated 10 November 2025). Accessed via: <data.gov.au/data/dataset/historical-migration-statistics/resource/b59a15df-86ea-4c4c-95be-4dd9fc9f8ac4>.

Chapter 6: Privatisation

1 **[Medicare has] raped the poor in this country . . .** From a doorstop interview with Leader of the Opposition John Howard, 1 June 1987. Accessed via: <parlinfo.aph.gov.au/parlInfo/download/media/pressrel/HPR09024510/upload_binary/HPR09024510.pdf>.

2 Ibid.

3 **Exempting the private health insurance rebate from income tax costs another $1.6 billion . . .** From Budget 2025–26. Accessed via: <budget.gov.au/content/bp1/download/bp1_2025-26.pdf>.

4 **Less than half of Australians have private health insurance . . .** From Greg Jericho, 'Private health insurance is a dud. That's why a majority of Australians don't have it', *The Guardian*, 12 November 2024, <theguardian.com/business/grogonomics/2024/nov/12/private-health-insurance-is-a-dud-thats-why-a-majority-of-australians-dont-have-it>.

5 **Federal funding to private schools increased by . . .** From Laura Penny and Emma Rowe, 'Yes, some Australian private schools are overfunded – here's why', The Conversation, 3 October 2016, <theconversation.com/yes-some-australian-private-schools-are-overfunded-heres-why-66212>.

6 **There has been a drop from 74 per cent in 1996 to . . .** From Sally Larsen, 'More Australian families are choosing private schools – we need to understand why', The Conversation, 17 December 2024, <theconversation.com/more-australian-families-are-choosing-private-schools-we-need-to-understand-why-242791>.

7 **Five private schools in New South Wales and Victoria spent more . . .** From 'Five private schools spent more on new facilities

than half the nations public schools in one year, union analysis finds', ABC News, 23 February 2024, <abc.net.au/news/2024-02-23/private-school-spending-education-union-report/103502588>.

8 **More spent on consulting and marketing . . .** From Joshua Black, 'Elective spending at Australian universities', The Australia Institute, 30 April 2025, <australiainstitute.org.au/report/elective-spending-at-australian-universities/>.

9 **The power to lift their fee caps . . .** From Juliet Breen, 'A deluge of debt: how HECS suffocates students', *Honi Soit*, 23 February 2024, <honisoit.com/2024/02/a-deluge-of-debt-how-hecs-suffocates-students/?utm_source=chatgpt.com>.

10 **Introduced tiers that changed how much you pay . . .** From 'Commonwealth Support for your Place and HECS-HELP – what you pay', Australian Government, Department of Education, Employment and Workplace Relations, 20 February 2010, <goingtouni.gov.au/Main/FeesLoansAndScholarships/Undergraduate/CommonwealthSupportForYourPlaceAndHECS-HELP/WhatYouPay.htm>.

11 **The system for setting university fees in the first place is broken . . .** From George Williams, 'Albanese's HECS relief won't fix the core problem – the fee system is broken', *Sydney Morning Herald*, 4 November 2024, <smh.com.au/national/albanese-s-hecs-relief-won-t-fix-the-core-problem-the-fees-system-is-broken-20241103-p5knfr.html>.

12 **The cost of doing a humanities degree at the University of Sydney increased by . . .** From Julie Hare, 'University funding model falls flat on all objectives: expert', *Australian Financial Review*, 3 January 2023, <afr.com/policy/health-and-education/university-funding-model-falls-on-all-objectives-expert-20230102-p5c9ye>.

13 **The last year before Howard finally got his voluntary student unionism bill . . .** From 'Joyce blasts colleagues over VSU vote', 10 December 2005, <abc.net.au/news/2005-12-10/joyce-blasts-colleagues-over-vsu-vote/758564>.

14 **Which ANU attempted to fully privatise . . .** From Sarah Lansdown, 'Beloved ANU childcare centres offered a fresh start after closure threat', *Canberra Times*, 22 February 2025, <canberratimes.com.au/story/8896766/new-beginnings-for-two-anu-early-learning-centres/>.

15 **HECS fees have increased by between 33 per cent and . . .** From 'Howard's clever country: make 'em pay more for less at university', *Sydney Morning Herald*, 27 April 2004, <smh.com.au/opinion/howards-clever-country-make-em-pay-more-for-less-at-university-20040427-gditi4.html>.

16 **The average HECS debt held by students has doubled . . .** From Joshua Black, *Elective Spending at Australian Universities (Discussion Paper)*, The Australia Institute, October 2024, <australiainstitute.org.au/wp-content/uploads/2024/11/P1736-University-is-expensive-Web-1.pdf>.

17 **Vocational education and training was cut by 24 per cent . . .** From Phil Bradley, 'Education funding and skills crisis', Green Left, 17 November 1993, <greenleft.org.au/content/education-funding-and-skills-crisis>.

18 **His policies helped create a shortage . . .** From Australian National Audit Office's 'Design and Implementation of the Australian Apprenticeships Incentive System'. Available via: <anao.gov.au/work/performance-audit/design-and-implementation-the-australian-apprenticeships-incentive-system>.

19 **Labor had started the market-led process for childcare . . .** From Deborah Brennan and Mab Oloman, 'Child Care in Australia: A market failure and spectacular public policy disaster', 2009, Canadian Centre for Policy Alternatives (Australian Office). Available via: <policyalternatives.ca/sites/default/files/uploads/publications/National%20Office/2009/04/Child%20Care%20in%20Australia.pdf>.

20 **Funding for private providers began in the 1960s . . .** From Gareth Hutchens, 'Privatising child care and aged care promised lower costs, more choice. Experts say some consequences are "devasting"', ABC News, 22 March 2025

21 **The average aged care home was funded for . . .** From Rick Morton, 'The collapse of aged care (part one and part two)', *The Saturday Paper/Get Up*, 18 September 2020, <cdn.getup.org.au/2769-The_collapse_of_aged_care_(part_one_and_two)_The_Saturday_Paper.pdf>.

22 **The profit share of residential care places increased . . .** From Gabrielle Meagher, 'A Genealogy of Aged Care', *Arena Quarterly*, No.6, June 2021, <arena.org.au/a-genealogy-of-aged-care/>.

23 **It was discovered that fifty-seven residents had been given diluted kerosene baths . . .** From 'Kerosene bath: Nurses banned', *The Age*, 29 March 2002, <theage.com.au/national/kerosene-bath-nurses-banned-20020329-gdu35d.html>.

24 **There were no regulations around restraints . . .** From Anne Connolly and John Stewart, 'Aged care home resident strapped to chair for total of 14 hours in one day', ABC News, 16 January 2019, <abc.net.au/news/2019-01-16/elderly-dementia-patients-given-anti-psychotics-and-restrained/10621658>.

25 **He wasn't helping to cinch Howard the numbers he needed . . .** 'Barnaby clears the way for Telstra sale', *Sydney Morning Herald*, 25 August 2005, <smh.com.au/national/barnaby-clears-the-way-for-telstra-sale-20050825-gdlxza.html>.

26 **Governments are bad at running businesses . . .** From Prime Minister John Howard in 'Telstra sale is a promise kept: Howard', *Sydney Morning Herald*, 26 August 2006, <smh.com.au/national/telstra-sale-is-a-promise-kept-howard-20060826-gdo9fk.html>.

27 **Paying Telstra to fix that copper network . . .** From *Australian Associated Press*, 'Telstra to be paid to fix copper network it sold to NBN for $11bn under new contract', *The Guardian*, 21 December 2015, <theguardian.com/business/2015/dec/21/telstras-nbn-contract-win-will-pay-telco-to-fix-copper-network-it-sold-for-11bn>.

Chapter 7: Revenue and Managing the Economy

1 **He's just got to wake up every morning and take credit for the outcomes I created . . .** A comment from Paul Keating to then Labor MP Mark Latham at lunch in 1999. As quoted in David Day, 'The election loss that still haunts Paul Keating', *Sydney Morning Herald*, 29 January 2015, <smh.com.au/lifestyle/the-election-loss-that-still-haunts-paul-keating-20150115-12r51d.html>.

2 **Inflation was running at 11 per cent . . .** From Economic Roundup, Summer 2004–05. Accessed via: <treasury.gov.au/sites/default/files/2019-03/full-1.pdf>.

3 **I'm not making that up, it's not a scare tactic . . .** Prime Minister John Howard in an interview with Steve Liebmann on the *Today Show*, Channel Nine, 30 August 2004. Accessed via: <pmtranscripts.pmc.gov.au/release/transcript-21499>.

4 **The Howard treasurership was not a success . . .** Peter Costello to the authors Wayne Errington and Peter van Onselen, quoted in Peter Hartcher, 'Howard failed as treasurer, says Costello', *Sydney Morning Herald*, 19 July 2007, <smh.com.au/national/howard-failed-as-treasurer-says-costello-20070719-gdqnhj.html>.

5 **It wasn't Howard who caused the price of Australian coal to rise . . .** Statistics from the World Bank 'Pink Sheet'. Accessed via: <worldbank.org/en/research/commodity-markets>.

6 Author's personal correspondence with Greg Jericho.

7 **Over two-thirds of the 5 percentage points . . .** Quote from Parliamentary Budget Office, 'Estimates of the structural budget balance of the Australian Government 2001–02 to 2016–17'. Accessed via: <pbo.gov.au/publications-and-data/publications/research-reports/estimates-structural-budget-balance-australian-government>.

8 Author's personal correspondence with Greg Jericho.

Chapter 8: Climate

1 **I've become a climate change agnostic . . .** John Howard in an interview with Sharri Markson for Sky News, 8 September 2025. Quoted in Oscar Godsell, 'Former prime minister John Howard declares net zero efforts "not worth the price we're paying"', Sky News, 8 September 2025, <skynews.com.au/australia-news/politics/former-prime-minister-john-howard-declares-net-zero-not-worth-the-price-were-paying/news-story/9285e1ce29838bfe84f30f6b58d0a899>.

2 **The then–Labor government was against taxing fossil fuels . . .** From Anne Davies, 'Cabinet papers: Keating MPs considered carbon tax to tackle climate change', *The Guardian*, 1 January 2018, <theguardian.com/australia-news/2018/jan/01/cabinet-papers-keating-mps-considered-carbon-tax-to-tackle-climate-change>.

3 **It is foolish to believe that we can continue to grow . . .** From Senator and Minister for Environment Robert Hill in a media release, 'Greenhouse Gas Figures Reveal Uniform Target Danger', 26 September 1997. Accessed via: <parlinfo.aph.gov.au/parlInfo/search/display/display.w3p;query=Id%3A%22media%2Fpressrel%2F2972326%22>.

4 **Howard's first climate plan . . .** From Matt Saunders and Richard Denniss, 'Overpromise and underdeliver – A brief history of

Australian climate plans', The Australia Institute, November 2021, <australiainstitute.org.au/wp-content/uploads/2021/11/Howards-Technology-Not-Taxes-WEB.pdf>.

5 Ibid.

6 **It is not in Australia's interest to ratify . . .** Prime Minister John Howard in an address to parliament in Canberra, 5 June 2002, as quoted in 'Australia rejects Kyoto Protocol', European Commission, 6 June 2002, <cordis.europa.eu/article/id/18505-australia-rejects-kyoto-protocol>.

7 **Emissions from actual economic activity have barely fallen . . .** From 'LULUCF explained: Why Australia's emissions aren't actually going down', The Australia Institute, 10 September 2024, <australiainstitute.org.au/post/lulucf-explained-why-australias-emissions-arent-actually-going-down/>.

8 **We just stopped clearing as much land or planted more trees . . .** From Clive Hamilton and Lins Vellen, 'Land-use change in Australia and the Kyoto Protocol', Environmental Science & Policy, Volume 2, Issue 2, May 1999, <sciencedirect.com/science/article/abs/pii/S1462901199000076>.

9 **The most cost-effective path . . .** Daniel Hurst, 'Sliding doors: cabinet papers reveal how close Coalition came to endorsing emissions trading in 2003, *The Guardian*, 1 January 2024, <theguardian.com/australia-news/2024/jan/01/liberal-coalition-cabinet-papers-emissions-trading-scheme-2003>.

10 **Recommends the government consider an emissions trading scheme . . .** From Daniel Hurst, 'Sliding doors: cabinet papers reveal how close Coalition came to endorsing emissions trading in 2003', *Guardian Australia*, 1 January 2024, <theguardian.com/australia-news/2024/jan/01/liberal-coalition-cabinet-papers-emissions-trading-scheme-2003>.

11 **I don't take policy advice from films . . .** Quote from John Howard in reference to *An Inconvenient Truth*, from 'Gore Visit to Push for Kyoto', *Sydney Morning Herald*, 4 May 2003, <smh.com.au/national/gore-visit-to-push-for-kyoto-20030504-gdgpdx.html>.

12 ***On the Waterfront* . . .** Prime Minister John Howard in an interview with Kerri-Anne Kennerley on *Midday*, Channel Nine, 19 February 1998. Accessed via: <pmtranscripts.pmc.gov.au/release/transcript-10704>.

13 **Extremely limited beneficial value to conservation . . .** From Dr Clive Hamilton in a government study, as quoted in a media release, 'Bald Hills Hypocrisy', The Australia Institute, 6 April 2006. Accessed via: <australiainstitute.org.au/wp-content/uploads/2020/12/MR216_8.pdf>.

14 **There are once again concerns about the impact a windfarm may have on the parrot . . .** From Adam Morton, 'Orange-bellied parrots have swelled back from imminent extinction – but now they face a new threat', *The Guardian*, 11 October 2025, <theguardian.com/environment/2025/oct/11/orange-bellied-parrots-have-swelled-back-from-imminent-extinction-but-now-they-face-a-new-threat>.

15 ***Four Corners* ran a story claiming scientists at the CSIRO . . .** *Four Corners* story quoted in Judy Skatssoon, 'Censorship "just the tip of the iceberg"', ABC Science, 14 February 2006, <abc.net.au/science/articles/2006/02/14/1569599.htm>.

16 **Abbott cut about $110 million from the CSIRO budget . . .** From Conor Duffy, 'CSIRO has "cut into the bone" to implement successive government cuts, chairman says', ABC News, 12 December 2014, <abc.net.au/news/2014-12-12/csiro-cut-to-the-bone-after-funding-cuts/5963994>.

17 **Advise on the nature and design of a workable global emissions trading system . . .** Prime Minister John Howard in an announcement on the Prime Ministerial Task Group on Emissions Trading, 10 December 2006. Accessed via: <pmtranscripts.pmc.gov.au/release/transcript-22624>.

18 **A proposal Turnbull put forward to join the agreement . . .** From 'Turnbull not denying reported support for Kyoto', ABC News, 28 October 2007, <abc.net.au/news/2007-10-28/turnbull-not-denying-reported-support-for-kyoto/2567324>.

19 **Which he then took to the 2007 election as Liberal policy . . .** Prime Ministerial Task Group on Emissions Trading – Final Report, 10 December 2006, <pmc.gov.au/publications/emissions/index.html>.

20 **The ETS was to start no later than 2012 . . .** Prime Minister John Howard in an address to Liberal Party Federal Council, Sydney, Press release, 3 June 2007. Accessed via: <parlinfo.aph.gov.au/parlInfo/search/display/display.w3p;query=Id:%22media/pressrel/IU9N6%22>.

21 **Started on a carbon pollution reduction scheme . . .** Prime Minister John Howard in a speech at the launch of the Australian Government's white paper on the Carbon Pollution Reduction Scheme, Canberra, 15 December 2008. Accessed via: <parlinfo.aph.gov.au/parlInfo/search/display/display.w3p;query=Id%3A%22media%2Fpressrel%2FLNES6%22>.

22 **Which was also designed to reduce carbon emissions . . .** From Christopher Knaus, 'The Liberal party is self-destructing over energy. Here's what you need to know', *The Guardian*, 20 August 2018, <theguardian.com/australia-news/2018/aug/20/liberal-party-self-destructing-national-energy-guarantee-malcolm-turnbull-what-you-need-to-know>.

23 **He first admitted this was based not on science . . .** From 'Howard defends actions on Kyoto protocol', ABC News, 8 December 2008, <abc.net.au/news/2008-12-08/howard-defends-actions-on-kyoto-protocol/233148>.

24 **He admitted that the only book he had read on climate change was . . .** From Nick Miller, '"The claims are exaggerated": John Howard rejects predictions of global warming catastrophe', *Sydney Morning Herald*, 6 November 2013, <smh.com.au/politics/federal/the-claims-are-exaggerated-john-howard-rejects-predictions-of-global-warming-catastrophe-20131106-2wzza.html>.

25 **I am unconvinced that catastrophe is around the corner . . .** Alexander White, 'Are most Australians really climate "agnostics"?', *The Guardian*, 20 January 2014, <theguardian.com/environment/southern-crossroads/2014/jan/19/australia-john-howard-climate-change-attitudes-polling-agnostics>.

26 See Nick Miller, '"The claims were exaggerated"'

27 **I think some aspects of the debate have become greatly exaggerated . . .** John Howard in a statement for ABC quoted in Graham Readfearn, 'John Howard's climate doubts reveal more about conservative identity politics than anything else', *The Guardian*, 4 August 2022, <theguardian.com/environment/2022/aug/04/john-howards-climate-doubts-reveal-more-about-conservative-identity-politics-than-anything-else>.

28 **Technology in the pipeline . . .** From Ray Noble, '"The Australian Way": how Morrison trashed brand Australia at COP26', The Conversation, 12 November 2021, <theconversation.com/

the-australian-way-how-morrison-trashed-brand-australia-at-cop26-171670>.

29 **We still have a massive fossil fuel problem . . .** From Emma Lovell and Jessica Allen, 'Australia's latest emissions data reveal we still have a giant fossil fuel problem', UNSW Newsroom, 11 June 2025

30 **Early action [on climate] would be more costly . . .** Brian Fisher to the Howard government as quoted in Andrew Macintosh, 'Domestic Influences on the Howard Government's Climate Policy: Using the Past as a Guide to the Future', *AsiaPacific Journal of Environmental Law*, Vol. 2008/4, 2008, <www7.austlii.edu.au/au/journals/AsPacJlEnvLaw/2008/4.pdf>.

31 **Fisher was hired by the Morrison government . . .** From Mike Foley, 'Author of Labor "wrecking ball" report hired for government net zero modelling', *Sydney Morning Herald*, 25 October 2021, <smh.com.au/politics/federal/author-of-labor-wrecking-ball-report-hired-for-government-net-zero-modelling-20211025-p5931t.html>.

Chapter 9: America's Bitch

1 **My friends, let me say to you today . . .** Prime Minister John Howard in his speech to US Congress, quoted in 'Howard's speech to Congress', *Sydney Morning Herald*, 13 June 2002, <smh.com.au/national/howards-speech-to-congress-20020613-gdfd3h.html>.

2 **Later banned Australian and New Zealand lamb exports . . .** From 'Business: The Economy Oz fury at US lamb ban', BBC News, 9 July 1999, <news.bbc.co.uk/2/hi/business/390046.stm>.

3 **Its intelligence over the Timorese massacres . . .** From Anne Barker, 'Declassified intelligence documents shed light on 1999 Timor Leste independence', ABC News, 29 August 2019, <abc.net.au/news/2019-08-29/declassified-us-intelligence-documents-sheds-light-timor-leste/11459284>.

4 **He could see the smoke rising from his room at the Willard hotel . . .** John Howard in an interview with Richard Fidler for ABC, 'John Howard recounts being in Washington on September 11, 2001', ABC Listen, 6 September 2021, <abc.net.au/listen/programs/conversations/john-howard-9-11-washington-witness-up-close-america/13520490>.

5 **Dear Mr Present . . .** A letter from Prime Minister John Howard to President George W Bush, quoted in 'Chapter 5: 20 years since

9/11', *The Alliance at 70*, United States Studies Centre, 28 March 2022. Accessed via: <ussc.edu.au/books/the-alliance-at-70/chapter-5-20-years-since-911>.

6 **Being on the spot had a powerful effect on me . . .** John Howard in an interview with Michael Gordon for *The Age*, 'Howard: why I went to war', *The Age*, 10 September 2011, <smh.com.au/national/howard-why-i-went-to-war-20110909-1k21n.html>.

7 **The idea of invoking ANZUS came . . .** John Howard to Alexander Downer, quoted in Andrew Tillett, 'After 70 years, ANZUS faces its biggest challenge', *Australian Financial Review*, 28 August 2021, <afr.com/politics/federal/after-70-years-anzus-faces-its-biggest-challenge-20210826-p58m1e>.

8 Ibid.

9 See John Howard in an interview with Michael Gordon

10 **I think the military textbooks will be replete . . .** Prime Minister John Howard in an address with President Bush discussing Operation Iraqi Freedom, The Bush Ranch, Crawford, Texas, 3 May 2003. Accessed via: <georgewbush-whitehouse.archives.gov/news/releases/2003/05/20030503-1.html>.

11 **Invaded just a couple of months after the UN report . . .** From Robert E Kelley, 'Twenty years ago in Iraq, ignoring the expert weapons inspectors proved to be a fatal mistake', SIPRI, 9 March 2023, <sipri.org/commentary/essay/2023/twenty-years-ago-iraq-ignoring-expert-weapons-inspectors-proved-be-fatal-mistake>.

12 **By 2004, it was clear the reports were false . . .** From Julian Borger, 'There were no weapons of mass destruction in Iraq', *The Guardian*, 7 October 2004, <theguardian.com/world/2004/oct/07/usa.iraq1>.

13 **I felt embarrassed, I did . . .** John Howard in an interview with the Seven Network, quoted in Luke Royes, 'Former prime minister John Howard "embarrassed" by Iraq WMD intelligence; says Julia Gillard's misogyny speech was "nonsense"', ABC News, 22 September 2014, <abc.net.au/news/2014-09-22/howard-embarrassed-by-intelligence-that-iraq-had-wmds/5759132>.

14 **A secretive committee Howard set up . . .** From Daniel Hurst, 'Australia went to war in Iraq based on "oral reports" to cabinet from John Howard', *The Guardian*, 1 January 2024, <theguardian.com/australia-news/2024/jan/01/australia-went-to-war-in-iraq-based-on-oral-reports-to-cabinet-from-john-howard>.

15 **So Howard relied on . . .** From Bill Campbell and Chris Moraitis, 'Memorandum of advice to the Commonwealth government on the use of force against Iraq', May 2003, Melbourne Journal of International Law, Inc. Accessed via: <go.gale.com/ps/i.do?id=GALE%7CA108837721&sid=sitemap&v=2.1&it=r&p=EAIM&sw=w&userGroupName=anon%7Eeba0625d&aty=open-web-entry>.

16 **Give instructions to the heads of service . . .** From Charles Sampford and Margaret Palmer, 'The Constitutional Power to Make War: Domestic Legal Issues Raised By Australia's Action in Iraq', 16 June 2009, SSRN. Accessed via: <papers.ssrn.com/sol3/papers.cfm?abstract_id=3033384>.

17 **Conga line of suckholes . . .** 'When politics and diplomacy are a bad mix', *The Age*, 11 February 2003, <theage.com.au/opinion/when-politics-and-diplomacy-are-a-bad-mix-20030211-gdv7hb.html>.

18 **Latham was denounced in the Australian media . . .** 'US alliance no bed of roses for Mark and Tom', *Sydney Morning Herald*, 11 February 2003, <smh.com.au/opinion/us-alliance-no-bed-of-roses-for-mark-and-tom-20030211-gdg92v.html>.

19 **I believe in the American alliance . . .** From Robert Manne, 'Little America', *The Monthly*, March 2006 Issue, <themonthly.com.au/march-2006/essays/little-america>.

Chapter 10: IR and Wages

1 **I mean, these are not the battlers of the trade union movement . . .** Prime Minister John Howard in an interview with Kerri-Anne Kennerley on *Midday*, Channel Nine, 19 February 1998. Accessed via: <pmtranscripts.pmc.gov.au/release/transcript-10704>.

2 **Overhauling Australia's arbitration and centralised wage fixing system . . .** From Gareth Hutchens, 'There's been a "30-year war" against unions in Australia, and think-tanks have played a role', ABC News, 2 October 2022, <abc.net.au/news/2022-10-02/sally-mcmanus-actu-thirty-year-war-against-unions/101458318>.

3 **I think what they did this afternoon will be greeted with revulsion . . .** From *The Age*, 20 August 1996, <smh.com.au/politics/federal/from-the-archives-1996-anarchy-as-protesters-storm-parliament-house-20210813-p58ii2.html>.

4 **The ban on closed shops had opened the wharves up . . .** From Tom Connors, 'Farmers take fight to the waterfront', *The Financial*

Review, 19 December 1997, <afr.com/policy/economy/farmers-take-fight-to-the-waterfront-19971219-k7ttj>.

5 See Prime Minister John Howard in an interview with Kerri-Anne Kennerley on *Midday*

6 **The MUA retained the right to represent waterfront workers . . .** From Kirsti Melville, 'The 1998 waterfront dispute pitted workers against each other. Recruits from the wharves share their stories', ABC News, 14 March 2025, <abc.net.au/news/2025-03-14/waterfront-dispute-pitted-workers-against-each-other-recruits/105007704>.

7 **The prime minister has said he is not going to abuse the power . . .** Senator Ron Boswell, quoted in 'PM's clean sweep: Senate control', *Sydney Morning Herald*, 29 October 2004, <smh.com.au/national/pms-clean-sweep-senate-control-20041029-gdk06e.html>.

8 **When the government scrapped the test . . .** From Kristin van Barneveld, 'Australian Workplace Agreements under WorkChoices', *The Economics and Labour Relations Review*, 2006, <www5.austlii.edu.au/au/journals/ELRRev/2006/8.html>.

9 **WorkChoices also superseded state powers over industrial relations . . .** From the Australian Government WorkChoices Factsheet, 'WorkChoices and unions', 2006. Accessed via: <aph.gov.au/~/media/Estimates/Live/eet_ctte/estimates/bud_0607/dewr/w098-07att29.ashx>.

10 **With Kevin Rudd appearing young(ish) . . .** From Ben Spies-Butcher and Shaun Wilson, 'Election 2007: Did the union campaign succeed?', Macquarie University, February 2008, <australianreview.net/digest/2008/02/spies-butcher_wilson.html>.

11 **The number of self-employed people grew . . .** From Norman Abjorensen, 'The meaning of John Howard', *Inside Story*, 1 March 2016, <insidestory.org.au/the-meaning-of-john-howard/>.

12 **Average annualised wages grew . . .** Media release from Senator Hon Murray Watt, 'New data shows Labor's workplace relations reforms delivering higher wages', Ministers' Media Centre, 27 March 2025, <ministers.dewr.gov.au/watt/new-data-shows-labors-workplace-relations-reforms-delivering-higher-wages>.

13 **If wage growth had kept up with the historical average . . .** From Gareth Hutchens, 'How a "lost decade" of wage growth stopped young Australians from buying homes', 30 March 2025, <abc.net.

au/news/2025-03-30/lost-decade-young-australians-home-ownership-per-capita/105109248>.

14 **Union membership in the public sector remains low . . .** From Cameron Roles and Michael O'Donnell, 'The *Fair Work Act* and the Worker Voice in the Australian Public Service,' *Adelaide Law Review*, 2013, <classic.austlii.edu.au/au/journals/AdelLawRw/2013/6.html>.

Chapter 11: The Liberal Party

1 **I would describe myself as an economic liberal . . .** Prime Minister John Howard in an address to the Centre of Independent Studies, 14 November 1996. Accessed via: <pmtranscripts.pmc.gov.au/sites/default/files/original/00010170.pdf>.

2 Ibid.

3 **He wouldn't even write them down as diary entries . . .** From Glenn Milne, 'Costello v Howard: Downer repudiates Costello', ABC News, 27 October 2010, <abc.net.au/news/2010-10-27/downer_repudiates_costello/40520>.

Chapter 12: Welfare and Unemployment

1 **We have a solemn obligation to help those in our community . . .** From Prime Minister John Howard in an address at the official launch of Centrelink (Commonwealth Services Delivery Agency), The Great Hall, Parliament House, 24 September 1997. Accessed via: <pmtranscripts.pmc.gov.au/sites/default/files/original/00010503.pdf>.

2 **But by 1975, neoliberalism was taking hold . . .** From Gareth Hutchens, 'Why Australia isn't aiming for "full employment" anymore', ABC News, 1 November 2020, <abc.net.au/news/2020-11-01/why-wouldnt-governments-want-full-employment/12836424>.

3 **Social security language shifted from 'entitlements' . . .** From Mona Nikidehaghani, Corinne Corese and Freda Hui-Truscott, 'Accounting and pastoral power in Australian disability welfare reform', *Critical Perspective on Accounting*, Science Direct, October 2021. Accessed via: <sciencedirect.com/science/article/abs/pii/S1045235419300784>.

4 **Centrelink was set up to save the government money . . .** From Esther Scott, 'Centrelink: A Service Delivery Agency in Australia', Harvard Kennedy School, Case Program, 1 September 1999.

Accessed via: <case.hks.harvard.edu/centrelink-a-service-delivery-agency-in-australia/>.

5 See Prime Minister John Howard in an address at the official launch of Centrelink

6 **That has not improved . . .** From Anne Davies, 'When "mutual obligation" began: John Howard's paradigm shift on welfare', 1 January 2022, <theguardian.com/australia-news/2022/jan/01/where-mutual-obligation-began-john-howards-paradigm-shift-on-welfare>.

7 See Prime Minister John Howard in an address at the official launch of Centrelink

8 **The election of the government marked a paradigm shift . . .** Shaun Wilson and Nick Turnbull, 'Wedge Politics and Welfare Reform in Australia', 2001. Accessed via: <onlinelibrary.wiley.com/doi/epdf/10.1111/1467-8497.00235>.

9 Ibid.

10 **To leave people on welfare is cruelty . . .** Tony Abbott quoted in 'War Declared: On Australian Dole Recipients', The Squeeze Is On, Wayne Smith, *The Courier-Mail*, 10 July 1999, <ourcivilisation.com/decline/jobs/punish.htm>.

11 **If this particular group of people feel relaxed . . .** Mal Brough quoted in Greg Ansley, 'Canberra rounds on "cruisers, dole bludgers"', *New Zealand Herald*, 20 May 2002, <nzherald.co.nz/world/canberra-rounds-on-cruisers-dole-bludgers/67M7EK2EYTSABRAW36TCMKPFTA/>.

12 **The start of the mining boom in 2003 . . .** Paolo Mauro, Rafael Romeu, Ariel Binder, Asad Zaman, 'A Modern History of Fiscal Prudence and Profligacy', International Monetary Fund, January 2013. Accessed via: <imf.org/external/pubs/ft/wp/2013/charts/wp1305_chartbk.pdf>.

13 **It costs billions . . .** Shane Wright, 'The baby bonus worked – at $86,000 for each extra child', *Sydney Morning Herald*, 6 October 2025, <smh.com.au/politics/federal/the-baby-bonus-worked-at-86-000-for-each-extra-child-20251003-p5mzwe.html>.

14 **Social Ventures Australia . . .** Inquiry into Workforce Australia Employment Services, Parliament of Australia, <aph.gov.au/Parliamentary_Business/Committees/House/Former_Committees/Workforce_Australia_Employment_Services/WorkforceAustralia>.

15 **Despite a 650-page report . . .** Rebuilding Employment Servies: Final report on Workforce Australia Employment Services, Parliament of Australia, November 2023. Accessed via: <parlinfo.aph.gov.au/parlInfo/download/committees/reportrep/RB000017/toc_pdf/RebuildingEmploymentServices.pdf>.

Conclusion

1 **When I look back I think that most of things I wanted to do . . .** 'Howard admits to a few regrets as PM', *The Australian*, 30 May 2012, <theaustralian.com.au/news/latest-news/howard-admits-to-a-few-regrets-as-pm-/news-story/25c8f820d714adee971b8fa45038fbe9>.

2 Ibid.

3 **A key plank in John Howard's modus operandi . . .** Tim Dunlop, ''Til the landslide bought me down', The Future of Everything Substack, 16 October 2025, <tdunlop.substack.com/p/til-the-landslide-brought-me-down>.

4 **I've explained why . . .** Prime Minister John Howard in an interview with John Laws for 2UE Radio, 29 May 2000. Accessed via: <pmtranscripts.pmc.gov.au/release/transcript-22788>.

5 **The worst thing that could happen to the country . . .** From Mungo MacCallum, 'Quarterly Essay 16 Breach of Trust', *Quarterly Essay*, December 2004, <quarterlyessay.com.au/correspondence/correspondence-mungo-maccallum-0>.

Acknowledgements

The depth of research, thought and triple checking involved in this project would have sent me screaming if not for the amazing work of friends, family, colleagues and the hopeful, who held me together with caffeine, compassion and chocolate to make sure it became a reality.

Thank you to Ben Ball and Shannon Grey and all those at Simon & Schuster for the idea, the faith and the push. You're right – we do need more reflective conversations.

Immeasurable thank yous to Isaac, Glenn, Alice, Skye, Morgan, Polly, Jack, Grogs, Matt, Frank, Elinor, Josh, Dave, Allan, Emma, Rod, Angus, Stephen and everyone at The Australia Institute who helped with research, guidance, listening to my rants, fed me, gave me space and dropped little gifts at my desk as I yelled, 'what an absolute f**kery!' twenty times a day. To Dee, Kathy, Emily, Hannah, Alison and Pamela – we would all fall apart without you. Thank you to Drij for the 24/7 tech support and to Richard, Leanne, Anna and Ebony for . . . everything. You'll never know just how much it is appreciated.

Apologies for the absolute absence and never-ending gratitude to those who still love me despite how consumed I have been with all of this. Blythe, Yvonne, Sarah, Tegan, Sala, Anna, Nathanael, Amy, the Little Writing Room, Melinda, Jan, Steph, Paul, Dan, Mikey, Sally, Nadine, Katrina and everyone else who sent encouragement, memes or checked I was still alive. I love you all and can't imagine life without you. Even when you're annoying.

To Vanessa for her patience, Laura for her humour and guidance, Murph for her Murphness, Ellen for her compassionate frankness and Niki for her example and heart, thank you for the sounding boards, the thoughts and, when necessary, the disagreements. You all make me a better journalist and human.

Extra treats to my beloved kittahns, Stevie and George, for the late nights and early mornings company. And to Gareth and Wolf for always reminding me what we are fighting for and why.

And to anyone who wants something better, who feels left behind, frustrated, angry and motivated. You matter. We know what the problems are. Here's to solving them. A x

About the Author

Amy Remeikis is the Chief Political Analyst at The Australia Institute and a contributing editor for *The New Daily*. Amy is renowned for her incisive political commentary and extensive experience as a journalist, author and former political reporter for *Guardian Australia*. Amy regularly appears in national media and is celebrated for her powerful writing on gender, politics and social justice. Her work continues to influence public debate and policy discussions across Australia. She is the author of *On Reckoning*. *Where It All Went Wrong* is her second book.